MznLnx

Missing Links Exam Preps

Exam Prep for

Exploring Marketing Research

Zikmund & Babin, 9th Edition

The MznLnx Exam Prep is your link from the texbook and lecture to your exams.
The MznLnx Exam Preps are unauthorized and comprehensive reviews of your textbooks.

All material provided by MznLnx and Rico Publications (c) 2010
Textbook publishers and textbook authors do not particpate in or contribute to these reviews.

MznLnx

Rico
Publications

Exam Prep for Exploring Marketing Research
9th Edition
Zikmund & Babin

Publisher: Raymond Houge
Assistant Editor: Michael Rouger
Text and Cover Designer: Lisa Buckner
Marketing Manager: Sara Swagger
Project Manager, Editorial Production: Jerry Emerson
Art Director: Vernon Lowerui

Product Manager: Dave Mason
Editorial Assitant: Rachel Guzmanji
Pedagogy: Debra Long
Cover Image: Jim Reed/Getty Images
Text and Cover Printer: City Printing, Inc.
Compositor: Media Mix, Inc.

(c) 2010 Rico Publications
ALL RIGHTS RESERVED. No part of this work covered by the copyright may be reproduced or used in any form or by an means--graphic, electronic, or mechanical, including photocopying, recording, taping, Web distribution, information storage, and retrieval systems, or in any other manner--without the written permission of the publisher.

Printed in the United States
ISBN:

For more information about our products, contact us at:

Dave.Mason@RicoPublications.com

For permission to use material from this text or

product, submit a request online to:

Dave.Mason@RicoPublications.com

Contents

CHAPTER 1
The Role of Marketing Research — 1

CHAPTER 2
Information Systems and Knowledge Management — 8

CHAPTER 3
The Marketing Research Process — 16

CHAPTER 4
The Human Side of Marketing Research: Organizational and Ethical Issues — 22

CHAPTER 5
Problem Definition: Jump-Starting the Research Process — 32

CHAPTER 6
Qualitative Research Tools — 36

CHAPTER 7
Secondary Data Research in a Digital Age — 41

CHAPTER 8
Survey Research: An Overview — 48

CHAPTER 9
Survey Research: Basic Methods of Communication with Respondents — 52

CHAPTER 10
Observation — 55

CHAPTER 11
Experimental Research: An Overview — 58

CHAPTER 12
Test-Markets and Experimental Design — 65

CHAPTER 13
Measurement — 70

CHAPTER 14
Attitude Measurement — 75

CHAPTER 15
Questionnaire Design — 78

CHAPTER 16
Sampling Designs and Sampling Procedures — 84

CHAPTER 17
Determination of Sample Size: A Review of Statistical Theory — 89

CHAPTER 18
Fieldwork — 96

CHAPTER 19
Editing and Coding: Transforming Raw Data into Information — 100

CHAPTER 20
Basic Data Analysis: Descriptive Statistics — 103

Contents (Cont.)

CHAPTER 21
Univariate Statistical Analysis — 106

CHAPTER 22
Bivariate Statistical Analysis: Differences Between Two Variables — 112

CHAPTER 23
Bivariate Statistical Analysis: Measures of Association — 116

CHAPTER 24
Introducing Multivariate Statistical Analysis — 121

CHAPTER 25
Communicating Research Results: Research Report, Oral Presentation — 127

ANSWER KEY — 132

TO THE STUDENT

COMPREHENSIVE

The *MznLnx* Exam Prep series is designed to help you pass your exams. Editors at MznLnx review your textbooks and then prepare these practice exams to help you master the textbook material. Unlike study guides, workbooks, and practice tests provided by the texbook publisher and textbook authors, *MznLnx* gives you **all** of the material in each chapter in exam form, not just samples, so you can be sure to nail your exam.

MECHANICAL

The MznLnx Exam Prep series creates exams that will help you learn the subject matter as well as test you on your understanding. Each question is designed to help you master the concept. Just working through the exams, you gain an understanding of the subject--its a simple mechanical process that produces success.

INTEGRATED STUDY GUIDE AND REVIEW

MznLnx is not just a set of exams designed to test you, its also a comprehensive review of the subject content. Each exam question is also a review of the concept, making sure that you will get the answer correct without having to go to other sources of material. You learn as you go! Its the easiest way to pass an exam.

HUMOR

Studying can be tedious and dry. MznLnx's instructional design includes moderate humor within the exam questions on occassion, to break the tedium and revitalize the brain

Chapter 1. The Role of Marketing Research 1

1. _____ is defined by the American _____ Association as the activity, set of institutions, and processes for creating, communicating, delivering, and exchanging offerings that have value for customers, clients, partners, and society at large. The term developed from the original meaning which referred literally to going to market, as in shopping, or going to a market to sell goods or services.

_____ practice tends to be seen as a creative industry, which includes advertising, distribution and selling.

- a. Customer acquisition management
- b. Product naming
- c. Marketing
- d. Marketing myopia

2. _____ is a business discipline which is focused on the practical application of marketing techniques and the management of a firm's marketing resources and activities. Marketing managers are often responsible for influencing the level, timing, and composition of customer demand accepted definition of the term. In part, this is because the role of a marketing manager can vary significantly based on a business' size, corporate culture, and industry context.

- a. Performance-based advertising
- b. Door-to-door
- c. Business structure
- d. Marketing Management

3. A _____ is a collection of symbols, experiences and associations connected with a product, a service, a person or any other artifact or entity.

_____s have become increasingly important components of culture and the economy, now being described as 'cultural accessories and personal philosophies'.

Some people distinguish the psychological aspect of a _____ from the experiential aspect.

- a. Store brand
- b. Brandable software
- c. Brand equity
- d. Brand

4. The U.S. _____ is an agency of the United States Department of Health and Human Services and is responsible for regulating and supervising the safety of foods, dietary supplements, drugs, vaccines, biological medical products, blood products, medical devices, radiation-emitting devices, veterinary products, and cosmetics. The FDA also enforces section 361 of the Public Health Service Act and the associated regulations, including sanitation requirements on interstate travel as well as specific rules for control of disease on products ranging from pet turtles to semen donations for assisted reproductive medicine techniques.

The FDA is an agency within the United States Department of Health and Human Services responsible for protecting and promoting the nation's public health.

- a. Power III
- b. Food and Drug Administration
- c. 6-3-5 Brainwriting
- d. 180SearchAssistant

5. In statistics, analysis of variance (_____) is a collection of statistical models, and their associated procedures, in which the observed variance is partitioned into components due to different explanatory variables. In its simplest form _____ gives a statistical test of whether the means of several groups are all equal, and therefore generalizes Student's two-sample t-test to more than two groups.

There are three conceptual classes of such models:

1. Fixed-effects models assumes that the data came from normal populations which may differ only in their means. (Model 1)
2. Random effects models assume that the data describe a hierarchy of different populations whose differences are constrained by the hierarchy. (Model 2)
3. Mixed-effect models describe situations where both fixed and random effects are present. (Model 3)

In practice, there are several types of _____ depending on the number of treatments and the way they are applied to the subjects in the experiment:

- One-way _____ is used to test for differences among two or more independent groups. Typically, however, the one-way _____ is used to test for differences among at least three groups, since the two-group case can be covered by a T-test (Gossett, 1908.)

    a. ANOVA
    b. AMAX
    c. ACNielsen
    d. ADTECH

6. _____ is a mathematical science pertaining to the collection, analysis, interpretation or explanation, and presentation of data. It also provides tools for prediction and forecasting based on data. It is applicable to a wide variety of academic disciplines, from the natural and social sciences to the humanities, government and business.

    a. Type I error
    b. Statistics
    c. Median
    d. Null hypothesis

7. Consumer market research is a form of applied sociology that concentrates on understanding the behaviours, whims and preferences, of consumers in a market-based economy, and aims to understand the effects and comparative success of marketing campaigns. The field of consumer _____ as a statistical science was pioneered by Arthur Nielsen with the founding of the ACNielsen Company in 1923.

Thus _____ is the systematic and objective identification, collection, analysis, and dissemination of information for the purpose of assisting management in decision making related to the identification and solution of problems and opportunities in marketing.

  a. Focus group
  b. Marketing research process
  c. Marketing research
  d. Logit analysis

8. Procter is a surname, and may also refer to:

    - Bryan Waller Procter (pseud. Barry Cornwall), English poet
    - Goodwin Procter, American law firm
    - _____, consumer products multinational

a. Flyer   b. Black PRies
c. Convergent   d. Procter ' Gamble

9. _____ is the practice of individuals including commercial businesses, governments and institutions, facilitating the sale of their products or services to other companies or organizations that in turn resell them, use them as components in products or services they offer _____ is also called business-to-_____ for short. (Note that while marketing to government entities shares some of the same dynamics of organizational marketing, B2G Marketing is meaningfully different.)

a. Mass marketing   b. Disruptive technology
c. Law of disruption   d. Business marketing

10. _____ is a measure of the strength of a brand, product, service relative to competitive offerings. There is often a geographic element to the competitive landscape. In defining _____, you must see to what extent a product, brand, or firm controls a product category in a given geographic area.

a. Productivity   b. Market system
c. Discretionary spending   d. Market dominance

11. _____ is a form of marketing developed from direct response marketing campaigns conducted in the 1970's and 1980's which emphasizes customer retention and satisfaction, rather than a dominant focus on 'point of sale' transactions.

_____ differs from other forms of marketing in that it recognizes the long term value to the firm of keeping customers, as opposed to direct or 'Intrusion' marketing, which focuses upon acquisition of new clients by targeting majority demographics based upon prospective client lists.

_____ refers to long-term and mutually beneficial arrangement wherein both buyer and seller focus on value enhancement through the certain of more satisfying exchange.This approach attempts to transcend the simple purchase exchange process with customer to make more meaningful and richer contact by providing a more holistic, personalized purchase, and use orn consumption experience to create stronger ties.

a. Global marketing   b. Diversity marketing
c. Relationship marketing   d. Guerrilla Marketing

12. An _____ is the manufacturing of a good or service within a category. Although _____ is a broad term for any kind of economic production, in economics and urban planning _____ is a synonym for the secondary sector, which is a type of economic activity involved in the manufacturing of raw materials into goods and products.

There are four key industrial economic sectors: the primary sector, largely raw material extraction industries such as mining and farming; the secondary sector, involving refining, construction, and manufacturing; the tertiary sector, which deals with services (such as law and medicine) and distribution of manufactured goods; and the quaternary sector, a relatively new type of knowledge _____ focusing on technological research, design and development such as computer programming, and biochemistry.

a. ADTECH   b. Industry
c. ACNielsen   d. AMAX

13. _____ is a business management strategy aimed at embedding awareness of quality in all organizational processes. _____ has been widely used in manufacturing, education, call centers, government, and service industries, as well as NASA space and science programs.

When used together as a phrase, the three words in this expression have the following meanings:

- Total: Involving the entire organization, supply chain, and/or product life cycle
- Quality: With its usual definitions, with all its complexities
- Management: The system of managing with steps like Plan, Organize, Control, Lead, Staff, provisioning and organizing.

As defined by the International Organization for Standardization (ISO):

> '_____ is a management approach for an organization, centered on quality, based on the participation of all its members and aiming at long-term success through customer satisfaction, and benefits to all members of the organization and to society.' ISO 8402:1994

One major aim is to reduce variation from every process so that greater consistency of effort is obtained. (Royse, D., Thyer, B., Padgett D., ' Logan T., 2006)

In Japan, _____ comprises four process steps, namely:

1. Kaizen - Focuses on 'Continuous Process Improvement', to make processes visible, repeatable and measurable.
2. Atarimae Hinshitsu - The idea that 'things will work as they are supposed to' .
3. Kansei - Examining the way the user applies the product leads to improvement in the product itself.
4. Miryokuteki Hinshitsu - The idea that 'things should have an aesthetic quality' (for example, a pen will write in a way that is pleasing to the writer.)

_____ requires that the company maintain this quality standard in all aspects of its business. This requires ensuring that things are done right the first time and that defects and waste are eliminated from operations.

a. 180SearchAssistant
b. Total quality management
c. Power III
d. 6-3-5 Brainwriting

14. _____ is a business term meaning the market segment to which a particular good or service is marketed. It is mainly defined by age, gender, geography, socio-economic grouping, technographic, or any other combination of demographics. It is generally studied and mapped by an organization through lists and reports containing demographic information that may have an effect on the marketing of key products or services.

a. Distribution
b. Brando
c. Market specialization
d. Category Development Index

15. _____ can be regarded as an outcome of mental processes (cognitive process) leading to the selection of a course of action among several alternatives. Every _____ process produces a final choice. The output can be an action or an opinion of choice.

Chapter 1. The Role of Marketing Research 5

a. Decision making
c. Power III
b. 6-3-5 Brainwriting
d. 180SearchAssistant

16. The _____ is generally accepted as the use and specification of the four p's describing the strategic position of a product in the marketplace. One version of the origins of the _____ starts in 1948 when James Culliton said that a marketing decision should be a result of something similar to a recipe. This version continued in 1953 when Neil Borden, in his American Marketing Association presidential address, took the recipe idea one step further and coined the term 'Marketing-Mix'.
  a. Power III
  c. Marketing mix
  b. 180SearchAssistant
  d. 6-3-5 Brainwriting

17. _____ is one of the four Ps of the marketing mix. The other three aspects are product, promotion, and place. It is also a key variable in microeconomic price allocation theory.
  a. Relationship based pricing
  c. Price
  b. Competitor indexing
  d. Pricing

18. _____ is one of the four elements of marketing mix. An organization or set of organizations (go-betweens) involved in the process of making a product or service available for use or consumption by a consumer or business user.

The other three parts of the marketing mix are product, pricing, and promotion.

  a. Distribution
  c. Japan Advertising Photographers' Association
  b. Better Living Through Chemistry
  d. Comparison-Shopping agent

19. A _____ or logistics network is the system of organizations, people, technology, activities, information and resources involved in moving a product or service from supplier to customer. _____ activities transform natural resources, raw materials and components into a finished product that is delivered to the end customer. In sophisticated _____ systems, used products may re-enter the _____ at any point where residual value is recyclable.
  a. Demand chain management
  c. Purchasing
  b. Supply chain
  d. Supply chain network

20. _____ involves disseminating information about a product, product line, brand, or company. It is one of the four key aspects of the marketing mix. (The other three elements are product marketing, pricing, and distribution). P>_____ is generally sub-divided into two parts:

  - Above the line _____: Promotion in the media (e.g. TV, radio, newspapers, Internet and Mobile Phones) in which the advertiser pays an advertising agency to place the ad
  - Below the line _____: All other _____. Much of this is intended to be subtle enough for the consumer to be unaware that _____ is taking place. E.g. sponsorship, product placement, endorsements, sales _____, merchandising, direct mail, personal selling, public relations, trade shows

  a. Davie Brown Index
  c. Cashmere Agency
  b. Promotion
  d. Bottling lines

Chapter 1. The Role of Marketing Research

21. Human beings are also considered to be _____ because they have the ability to change raw materials into valuable _____. The term Human _____ can also be defined as the skills, energies, talents, abilities and knowledge that are used for the production of goods or the rendering of services. While taking into account human beings as _____, the following things have to be kept in mind:

- The size of the population
- The capabilities of the individuals in that population

Many _____ cannot be consumed in their original form. They have to be processed in order to change them into more usable commodities.

a. Power III
b. 180SearchAssistant
c. 6-3-5 Brainwriting
d. Resources

22. In probability theory and statistics, _____ indicates the strength and direction of a linear relationship between two random variables. That is in contrast with the usage of the term in colloquial speech, denoting any relationship, not necessarily linear. In general statistical usage, _____ or co-relation refers to the departure of two random variables from independence.

a. Mean
b. Frequency distribution
c. Probability
d. Correlation

23. _____ , according to The American Marketing Association, is 'a planning process designed to assure that all brand contacts received by a customer or prospect for a product, service, or organization are relevant to that person and consistent over time.' (Marketing Power Dictionary)

_____ is a term used to describe a holistic approach to marketing. It aims to ensure consistency of message and the complementary use of media. The concept includes online and offline marketing channels.

a. Integrated marketing communications
b. ADTECH
c. AMAX
d. ACNielsen

24. _____ refers to messages and related media used to communicate with a market. Those who practice advertising, branding, direct marketing, graphic design, marketing, packaging, promotion, publicity, public relations, sales, sales promotion and online marketing are termed marketing communicators, _____ managers, or more briefly as marcom managers.

a. Sales promotion
b. Merchandise
c. Merchandising
d. Marketing communication

25. A personal and cultural _____ is a relative ethic _____, an assumption upon which implementation can be extrapolated. A _____ system is a set of consistent _____s and measures that is soo not true. A principle _____ is a foundation upon which other _____s and measures of integrity are based.

a. Package-on-Package
b. Perceptual maps
c. Supreme Court of the United States
d. Value

26. The Oxford University Press defines _____ as 'marketing on a worldwide scale reconciling or taking commercial advantage of global operational differences, similarities and opportunities in order to meet global objectives.' Oxford University Press' Glossary of Marketing Terms.

Here are three reasons for the shift from domestic to _____ as given by the authors of the textbook, _____ Management--3rd Edition by Masaaki Kotabe and Kristiaan Helsen, 2004.

One of the product categories in which global competition has been easy to track is in U.S. automotive sales.

a. Digital marketing
c. Diversity marketing
b. Guerrilla Marketing
d. Global marketing

27. The _____ is an economic and political union of 27 member states, located primarily in Europe. It was established by the Treaty of Maastricht on 1 November 1993 upon the foundations of the pre-existing European Economic Community. With almost 500 million citizens, the _____ combined generates an estimated 30% share (US$16.8 trillion in 2007) of the nominal gross world product.

a. European Union
c. Eurozone
b. ADTECH
d. ACNielsen

Chapter 2. Information Systems and Knowledge Management

1. _____ refer to a collection of facts usually collected as the result of experience, observation or experiment or a set of premises. This may consist of numbers, words particularly as measurements or observations of a set of variables. _____ are often viewed as a lowest level of abstraction from which information and knowledge are derived.
   a. Sample size
   b. Pearson product-moment correlation coefficient
   c. Data
   d. Mean

2. _____ is defined by the American _____ Association as the activity, set of institutions, and processes for creating, communicating, delivering, and exchanging offerings that have value for customers, clients, partners, and society at large. The term developed from the original meaning which referred literally to going to market, as in shopping, or going to a market to sell goods or services.

   _____ practice tends to be seen as a creative industry, which includes advertising, distribution and selling.

   a. Marketing
   b. Product naming
   c. Marketing myopia
   d. Customer acquisition management

3. A _____ is a process that can allow an organization to concentrate its limited resources on the greatest opportunities to increase sales and achieve a sustainable competitive advantage. A _____ should be centered around the key concept that customer satisfaction is the main goal.

   A _____ is most effective when it is an integral component of corporate strategy, defining how the organization will successfully engage customers, prospects, and competitors in the market arena.

   a. Marketing strategy
   b. Psychographic
   c. Cyberdoc
   d. Societal marketing

4. A _____ is a plan of action designed to achieve a particular goal.

   _____ is different from tactics. In military terms, tactics is concerned with the conduct of an engagement while _____ is concerned with how different engagements are linked.

   a. 6-3-5 Brainwriting
   b. 180SearchAssistant
   c. Strategy
   d. Power III

5. _____ comprises a range of practices used in an organisation to identify, create, represent, distribute and enable adoption of insights and experiences. Such insights and experiences comprise knowledge, either embodied in individuals or embedded in organisational processes or practice. An established discipline since 1991, _____ includes courses taught in the fields of business administration, information systems, management, and library and information sciences.
   a. Knowledge management
   b. Power III
   c. 6-3-5 Brainwriting
   d. 180SearchAssistant

6. Radio-frequency identification (_____) is the use of an object (typically referred to as an _____ tag) applied to or incorporated into a product, animal, or person for the purpose of identification and tracking using radio waves. Some tags can be read from several meters away and beyond the line of sight of the reader.

   Most _____ tags contain at least two parts.

a. 6-3-5 Brainwriting
c. 180SearchAssistant
b. Power III
d. RFID

7. _____ is an advertisement in which a particular product specifically mentions a competitor by name for the express purpose of showing why the competitor is inferior to the product naming it.

This should not be confused with parody advertisements, where a fictional product is being advertised for the purpose of poking fun at the particular advertisement, nor should it be confused with the use of a coined brand name for the purpose of comparing the product without actually naming an actual competitor. ('Wikipedia tastes better and is less filling than the Encyclopedia Galactica.')

In the 1980s, during what has been referred to as the cola wars, soft-drink manufacturer Pepsi ran a series of advertisements where people, caught on hidden camera, in a blind taste test, chose Pepsi over rival Coca-Cola.

a. Heavy-up
c. GL-70
b. Cost per conversion
d. Comparative advertising

8. _____ is the use of an object (typically referred to as an RFID tag) applied to or incorporated into a product, animal, or person for the purpose of identification and tracking using radio waves. Some tags can be read from several meters away and beyond the line of sight of the reader.

Most RFID tags contain at least two parts.

a. 6-3-5 Brainwriting
c. Power III
b. 180SearchAssistant
d. Radio-frequency identification

9. _____ is a business discipline which is focused on the practical application of marketing techniques and the management of a firm's marketing resources and activities. Marketing managers are often responsible for influencing the level, timing, and composition of customer demand accepted definition of the term. In part, this is because the role of a marketing manager can vary significantly based on a business' size, corporate culture, and industry context.

a. Business structure
c. Door-to-door
b. Performance-based advertising
d. Marketing Management

10. In probability theory and statistics, _____ indicates the strength and direction of a linear relationship between two random variables. That is in contrast with the usage of the term in colloquial speech, denoting any relationship, not necessarily linear. In general statistical usage, _____ or co-relation refers to the departure of two random variables from independence.

a. Probability
c. Mean
b. Correlation
d. Frequency distribution

11. Consumer market research is a form of applied sociology that concentrates on understanding the behaviours, whims and preferences, of consumers in a market-based economy, and aims to understand the effects and comparative success of marketing campaigns. The field of consumer _____ as a statistical science was pioneered by Arthur Nielsen with the founding of the ACNielsen Company in 1923 .

Chapter 2. Information Systems and Knowledge Management

Thus _____ is the systematic and objective identification, collection, analysis, and dissemination of information for the purpose of assisting management in decision making related to the identification and solution of problems and opportunities in marketing.

   a. Focus group
   b. Logit analysis
   c. Marketing research process
   d. Marketing research

12. Human beings are also considered to be _____ because they have the ability to change raw materials into valuable _____. The term Human _____ can also be defined as the skills, energies, talents, abilities and knowledge that are used for the production of goods or the rendering of services. While taking into account human beings as _____, the following things have to be kept in mind:

- The size of the population
- The capabilities of the individuals in that population

Many _____ cannot be consumed in their original form. They have to be processed in order to change them into more usable commodities.

   a. Resources
   b. 6-3-5 Brainwriting
   c. Power III
   d. 180SearchAssistant

13. A _____ is a structured collection of records or data that is stored in a computer system. The structure is achieved by organizing the data according to a _____ model. The model in most common use today is the relational model.

   a. 6-3-5 Brainwriting
   b. Power III
   c. 180SearchAssistant
   d. Database

14. The _____ is a global navigation satellite system (GNSS) developed by the United States Department of Defense and managed by the United States Air Force 50th Space Wing. It is the only fully functional GNSS in the world, can be used freely, and is often used by civilians for navigation purposes. It uses a constellation of between 24 and 32 Medium Earth Orbit satellites that transmit precise microwave signals, which allow _____ receivers to determine their current location, the time, and their velocity.

   a. Global positioning system
   b. 6-3-5 Brainwriting
   c. 180SearchAssistant
   d. Power III

15. _____ is a mathematical science pertaining to the collection, analysis, interpretation or explanation, and presentation of data. It also provides tools for prediction and forecasting based on data. It is applicable to a wide variety of academic disciplines, from the natural and social sciences to the humanities, government and business.

   a. Null hypothesis
   b. Median
   c. Type I error
   d. Statistics

16. A _____ is any statistical test for which the distribution of the test statistic under the null hypothesis can be approximated by a normal distribution. Since many test statistics are approximately normally distributed for large samples (due to the central limit theorem), many statistical tests can be performed as approximate _____s if the sample size is not too small. In addition, some statistical tests such as comparisons of means between two samples, or a comparison of the mean of one sample to a given constant, are exact _____s under certain assumptions.

Chapter 2. Information Systems and Knowledge Management

a. Null hypothesis
c. Sample size
b. Z-test
d. Confounding variables

17. In environmental modeling and especially in hydrology, a _____ model means a model that is acceptably consistent with observed natural processes, i.e. that simulates well, for example, observed river discharge. It is a key concept of the so-called Generalized Likelihood Uncertainty Estimation (GLUE) methodology to quantify how uncertain environmental predictions are.

a. Behavioral
c. 180SearchAssistant
b. Power III
d. 6-3-5 Brainwriting

18. _____ is a global marketing research firm, with worldwide headquarters in New York City. Regional headquarters for North America are located in Schaumburg, IL. As of 2008, its the part of The Nielsen Company.

a. E-Detailing
c. InfoNU
b. Alloy Entertainment
d. ACNielsen

19. In statistics, analysis of variance (_____) is a collection of statistical models, and their associated procedures, in which the observed variance is partitioned into components due to different explanatory variables. In its simplest form _____ gives a statistical test of whether the means of several groups are all equal, and therefore generalizes Student's two-sample t-test to more than two groups.

There are three conceptual classes of such models:

1. Fixed-effects models assumes that the data came from normal populations which may differ only in their means. (Model 1)
2. Random effects models assume that the data describe a hierarchy of different populations whose differences are constrained by the hierarchy. (Model 2)
3. Mixed-effect models describe situations where both fixed and random effects are present. (Model 3)

In practice, there are several types of _____ depending on the number of treatments and the way they are applied to the subjects in the experiment:

- One-way _____ is used to test for differences among two or more independent groups. Typically, however, the one-way _____ is used to test for differences among at least three groups, since the two-group case can be covered by a T-test (Gossett, 1908.)

a. ANOVA
c. ACNielsen
b. ADTECH
d. AMAX

20. The _____ is a publication of the United States Census Bureau, an agency of the United States Department of Commerce. Published annually since 1878, the statistics describe social and economic conditions in the United States.

In 1975 a two volume Historical Statistics of the United States, Colonial Times to 1970 Bicentennial Edition was published.

a. 6-3-5 Brainwriting
c. Power III
b. Statistical Abstract of the United States
d. 180SearchAssistant

21. An _____ is a special-purpose computer system designed to perform one or a few dedicated functions, often with real-time computing constraints. It is usually embedded as part of a complete device including hardware and mechanical parts. In contrast, a general-purpose computer, such as a personal computer, can do many different tasks depending on programming.
   a. ADTECH
   c. AMAX
   b. ACNielsen
   d. Embedded system

22. _____ is one of the four elements of marketing mix. An organization or set of organizations (go-betweens) involved in the process of making a product or service available for use or consumption by a consumer or business user.

The other three parts of the marketing mix are product, pricing, and promotion.

   a. Comparison-Shopping agent
   c. Japan Advertising Photographers' Association
   b. Distribution
   d. Better Living Through Chemistry

23. _____ refers to the structured transmission of data between organizations by electronic means. It is used to transfer electronic documents from one computer system to another (ie) from one trading partner to another trading partner. It is more than mere E-mail; for instance, organizations might replace bills of lading and even checks with appropriate _____ messages.
   a. AMAX
   c. ACNielsen
   b. ADTECH
   d. Electronic data interchange

24. _____ is a broad label that refers to any individuals or households that use goods and services generated within the economy. The concept of a _____ is used in different contexts, so that the usage and significance of the term may vary.

A _____ is a person who uses any product or service.

   a. 180SearchAssistant
   c. Consumer
   b. Power III
   d. 6-3-5 Brainwriting

25. In computing, a _____ is a type of Uniform Resource Identifier (URI) that specifies where an identified resource is available and the mechanism for retrieving it. In popular usage and in many technical documents and verbal discussions it is often incorrectly used as a synonym for URI. In popular language, a _____ is also referred to as a Web address.
   a. AMAX
   c. ACNielsen
   b. ADTECH
   d. Uniform Resource Locator

26. _____ is a process of gathering, analyzing, and dispensing information for tactical or strategic purposes. The _____ process entails obtaining both factual and subjective information on the business environments in which a company is operating or considering entering.

There are three ways of scanning the business environment:

- Ad-hoc scanning - Short term, infrequent examinations usually initiated by a crisis
- Regular scanning - Studies done on a regular schedule (say, once a year)
- Continuous scanning(also called continuous learning) - continuous structured data collection and processing on a broad range of environmental factors

Most commentators feel that in today's turbulent business environment the best scanning method available is continuous scanning.This allows the firm to :

-act quickly-take advantage of opportunities before competitors do-respond to environmental threats before significant damage is done

The Macro Environment

_____ usually refers just to the macro environment, but it can also include:-industry -competitor analysis -marketing research(consumer analysis) -New Product Development(product innovations)- the company's internal environment

Macro _____ involves analysing:

- The Economy

GDP per capitaeconomic growthunemployment]] rateinflation]] rateconsumer and investor confidenceinventory levelscurrency exchange ratesmerchandise trade balancefinancial and political health of trading partnersbalance of paymentsfuture trends

- Government

political climate - amount of government activitypolitical stability and riskgovernment debtbudget deficit or surpluscorporate and personal tax ratespayroll taxesimport tariffs and quotasexport restrictionsrestrictions on international financial flows

- Legal

minimum wage lawsenvironmental protection lawsworker safety lawsunion lawscopyright and patent lawsanti- monopoly lawsSunday closing lawsmunicipal licenceslaws that favour business investment

- Technology

efficiency of infrastructure, including: roads, ports, airports, rolling stock, hospitals, education, healthcare, communication, etc.industrial productivitynew manufacturing processesnew products and services of competitorsnew products and services of supply chain partnersany new technology that could impact the companycost and accessibility of electrical power

- Ecology
  - ecological concerns that affect the firms production processes
  - ecological concerns that affect customers' buying habits
  - ecological concerns that affect customers' perception of the company or product
- Socio-Cultural
  - demographic factors such as:
    - population size and distribution
    - age distribution
    - education levels
    - income levels
    - ethnic origins
    - religious affiliations
  - attitudes towards:
    - materialism, capitalism, free enterprise
    - individualism, role of family, role of government, collectivism
    - role of church and religion
    - consumerism
    - environmentalism
    - importance of work, pride of accomplishment
  - cultural structures including:
    - diet and nutrition
    - housing conditions
- Potential Suppliers
  - Labour supply
    - quantity of labour available
    - quality of labour available
    - stability of labour supply
    - wage expectations
    - employee turn-over rate
    - strikes and labour relations
    - educational facilities
  - Material suppliers
    - quality, quantity, price, and stability of material inputs
    - delivery delays
    - proximity of bulky or heavy material inputs
    - level of competition among suppliers
  - Service Providers
    - quantity, quality, price, and stability of service facilitators
    - special requirements
- Stakeholders
  - Lobbyists
  - Shareholders
  - Employees
  - Partners

Chapter 2. Information Systems and Knowledge Management

Scanning these macro environmental variables for threats and opportunities requires that each issue be rated on two dimensions. It must be rated on its potential impact on the company, and rated on its likeliness of occurrence.

a. AMAX
b. Environmental scanning
c. ADTECH
d. ACNielsen

27. The business terms _____ and pull originated in the logistic and supply chain management, but are also widely used in marketing.

A _____-pull-system in business describes the move of a product or information between two subjects. On markets the consumers usually 'pulls' the goods or information they demand for their needs, while the offerers or suppliers '_____es' them toward the consumers.

a. Gold Key Matching Service
b. Completely randomized designs
c. Manufacturers' representatives
d. Push

28. A _____ is defined by the International Co-operative Alliance's Statement on the Co-operative Identity as an autonomous association of persons united voluntarily to meet their common economic, social, and cultural needs and aspirations through a jointly-owned and democratically-controlled enterprise. It is a business organization owned and operated by a group of individuals for their mutual benefit. A _____ may also be defined as a business owned and controlled equally by the people who use its services or who work at it.

a. 6-3-5 Brainwriting
b. Power III
c. Cooperative
d. 180SearchAssistant

Chapter 3. The Marketing Research Process

1. _____ is that part of statistical practice concerned with the selection of individual observations intended to yield some knowledge about a population of concern, especially for the purposes of statistical inference. Each observation measures one or more properties (weight, location, etc.) of an observable entity enumerated to distinguish objects or individuals.
   a. Sports Marketing Group
   b. AStore
   c. Richard Buckminster 'Bucky' Fuller
   d. Sampling

2. The United States _____ is the government agency that is responsible for the United States Census. It also gathers other national demographic and economic data.
   a. Power III
   b. Census Bureau
   c. 6-3-5 Brainwriting
   d. 180SearchAssistant

3. _____ can be regarded as an outcome of mental processes (cognitive process) leading to the selection of a course of action among several alternatives. Every _____ process produces a final choice. The output can be an action or an opinion of choice.
   a. Power III
   b. 180SearchAssistant
   c. Decision making
   d. 6-3-5 Brainwriting

4. _____ refer to a collection of facts usually collected as the result of experience, observation or experiment or a set of premises. This may consist of numbers, words particularly as measurements or observations of a set of variables. _____ are often viewed as a lowest level of abstraction from which information and knowledge are derived.
   a. Pearson product-moment correlation coefficient
   b. Mean
   c. Sample size
   d. Data

5. Procter is a surname, and may also refer to:

   - Bryan Waller Procter (pseud. Barry Cornwall), English poet
   - Goodwin Procter, American law firm
   - _____, consumer products multinational

   a. Procter ' Gamble
   b. Flyer
   c. Black PRies
   d. Convergent

6. _____ describes data and characteristics about the population or phenomenon being studied. _____ answers the questions who, what, where, when and how.

Although the data description is factual, accurate and systematic, the research cannot describe what caused a situation.

   a. Descriptive research
   b. Sampling error
   c. Power III
   d. Two-tailed test

Chapter 3. The Marketing Research Process

7. In business and engineering, new _____ is the term used to describe the complete process of bringing a new product or service to market. There are two parallel paths involved in the Nproduct development process: one involves the idea generation, product design, and detail engineering; the other involves market research and marketing analysis. Companies typically see new _____ as the first stage in generating and commercializing new products within the overall strategic process of product life cycle management used to maintain or grow their market share.
   a. Specification tree
   b. New product development
   c. New product screening
   d. Product development

8. A personal and cultural _____ is a relative ethic _____, an assumption upon which implementation can be extrapolated. A _____ system is a set of consistent _____s and measures that is soo not true. A principle _____ is a foundation upon which other _____s and measures of integrity are based.
   a. Value
   b. Perceptual maps
   c. Package-on-Package
   d. Supreme Court of the United States

9. _____ is a broad label that refers to any individuals or households that use goods and services generated within the economy. The concept of a _____ is used in different contexts, so that the usage and significance of the term may vary.

   A _____ is a person who uses any product or service.

   a. Power III
   b. 6-3-5 Brainwriting
   c. Consumer
   d. 180SearchAssistant

10. A _____ is a structured collection of records or data that is stored in a computer system. The structure is achieved by organizing the data according to a _____ model. The model in most common use today is the relational model.
    a. 6-3-5 Brainwriting
    b. Power III
    c. Database
    d. 180SearchAssistant

11. _____ is a telephone surveying technique in which the interviewer follows a script provided by a software application. The software is able to customize the flow of the questionnaire based on the answers provided, as well as information already known about the participant.

Chapter 3. The Marketing Research Process

CATI may function in the following manner

- A computerized questionnaire is administered to respondents over the telephone.
- The interviewer sits in front of a computer screen
- Upon command, the computer dials the telephone number to be called.
- When contact is made, the interviewer reads the questions posed on the computer screen and records the respondent's answers directly into the computer.
- Interim and update reports can be compiled instantaneously, as the data are being collected.
- CATI software has built-in logic, which also enhances data accuracy.
- The program will personalize questions and control for logically incorrect answers, such as percentage answers that do not add up to 100 percent.
- The software has built-in branching logic, which will skip questions that are not applicable or will probe for more detail when warranted.

a. 180SearchAssistant
b. Power III
c. 6-3-5 Brainwriting
d. Computer-assisted telephone interviewing

12. _____ denotes a necessary relationship between one event and another event (called effect) which is the direct consequence of the first.

While this informal understanding suffices in everyday use, the philosophical analysis of how best to characterize _____ extends over millennia. In the western philosophical tradition explicit discussion stretches back at least as far as Aristotle, and the topic remains a staple in contemporary philosophy journals.

a. Causality
b. 6-3-5 Brainwriting
c. Power III
d. 180SearchAssistant

13. _____ is an advertisement in which a particular product specifically mentions a competitor by name for the express purpose of showing why the competitor is inferior to the product naming it.

This should not be confused with parody advertisements, where a fictional product is being advertised for the purpose of poking fun at the particular advertisement, nor should it be confused with the use of a coined brand name for the purpose of comparing the product without actually naming an actual competitor. ('Wikipedia tastes better and is less filling than the Encyclopedia Galactica.')

In the 1980s, during what has been referred to as the cola wars, soft-drink manufacturer Pepsi ran a series of advertisements where people, caught on hidden camera, in a blind taste test, chose Pepsi over rival Coca-Cola.

a. Comparative advertising
b. Heavy-up
c. GL-70
d. Cost per conversion

14. _____s are used in open sentences. For instance, in the formula x + 1 = 5, x is a _____ which represents an 'unknown' number. _____s are often represented by letters of the Roman alphabet, or those of other alphabets, such as Greek, and use other special symbols.
    a. Book of business
    b. Personalization
    c. Quantitative
    d. Variable

15. _____ is a type of research conducted because a problem has not been clearly defined. _____ helps determine the best research design, data collection method and selection of subjects. Given its fundamental nature, _____ often concludes that a perceived problem does not actually exist.
    a. Exploratory research
    b. Intent scale translation
    c. IDDEA
    d. ACNielsen

16. _____ is a computer program used for statistical analysis.

_____ (originally, Statistical Package for the Social Sciences) was released in its first version in 1968 after being founded by Norman Nie and C. Hadlai Hull. Nie was then a political science postgraduate at Stanford University,and now Research Professor in the Department of Political Science at Stanford and Professor Emeritus of Political Science at the University of Chicago.

    a. 6-3-5 Brainwriting
    b. Power III
    c. 180SearchAssistant
    d. SPSS

17. _____ is a mathematical science pertaining to the collection, analysis, interpretation or explanation, and presentation of data. It also provides tools for prediction and forecasting based on data. It is applicable to a wide variety of academic disciplines, from the natural and social sciences to the humanities, government and business.
    a. Null hypothesis
    b. Type I error
    c. Median
    d. Statistics

18. In probability theory and statistics, _____ indicates the strength and direction of a linear relationship between two random variables. That is in contrast with the usage of the term in colloquial speech, denoting any relationship, not necessarily linear. In general statistical usage, _____ or co-relation refers to the departure of two random variables from independence.
    a. Correlation
    b. Mean
    c. Probability
    d. Frequency distribution

19. A _____ is a form of qualitative research in which a group of people are asked about their attitude towards a product, service, concept, advertisement, idea, or packaging. Questions are asked in an interactive group setting where participants are free to talk with other group members.

Ernest Dichter originated the idea of having a 'group therapy' for products and this process is what became known as a _____.

    a. Marketing research process
    b. Cross tabulation
    c. Logit analysis
    d. Focus group

Chapter 3. The Marketing Research Process

20. _____ in organizations and public policy is both the organizational process of creating and maintaining a plan; and the psychological process of thinking about the activities required to create a desired goal on some scale. As such, it is a fundamental property of intelligent behavior. This thought process is essential to the creation and refinement of a plan, or integration of it with other plans, that is, it combines forecasting of developments with the preparation of scenarios of how to react to them.

   a. Planning
   b. Power III
   c. 180SearchAssistant
   d. 6-3-5 Brainwriting

21. A number of different _____s are indicated below.

   - Randomized controlled trial
     - Double-blind randomized trial
     - Single-blind randomized trial
     - Non-blind trial
   - Nonrandomized trial (quasi-experiment)
     - Interrupted time series design (measures on a sample or a series of samples from the same population are obtained several times before and after a manipulated event or a naturally occurring event) - considered a type of quasi-experiment

   - Cohort study
     - Prospective cohort
     - Retrospective cohort
     - Time series study
   - Case-control study
     - Nested case-control study
   - Cross-sectional study
     - Community survey (a type of cross-sectional study)

   When choosing a _____, many factors must be taken into account. Different types of studies are subject to different types of bias. For example, recall bias is likely to occur in cross-sectional or case-control studies where subjects are asked to recall exposure to risk factors.

   a. Study design
   b. 180SearchAssistant
   c. Longitudinal studies
   d. Power III

22. A _____ is a tool used to measure the viewing habits of TV and cable audiences.

   The _____ is a 'box', about the size of a paperback book. The box is hooked up to each television set and is accompanied by a remote control unit.

   a. 180SearchAssistant
   b. 6-3-5 Brainwriting
   c. Power III
   d. People meter

23. _____ is a process of gathering, modeling, and transforming data with the goal of highlighting useful information, suggesting conclusions, and supporting decision making. _____ has multiple facets and approaches, encompassing diverse techniques under a variety of names, in different business, science, and social science domains.

Data mining is a particular _____ technique that focuses on modeling and knowledge discovery for predictive rather than purely descriptive purposes.

a. 180SearchAssistant
b. Data analysis
c. Power III
d. 6-3-5 Brainwriting

24. Combining Existing _____ Sources with New Primary Data Sources

Imagine that we could get hold of a good collection of surveys taken in earlier years, such as detailed studies about changes going on in this phase and hopefully additional studies in the years to come. Analyzing this data base over time could give us a good picture of what changes actually have taken place in the orientation of the population and of the extent to which new technical concepts did have an impact on subgroups of the population. Furthermore, data archives can help to prepare studies on change over time by monitoring what questions have been asked in earlier years and alerting principal investigators to important questions which should be repeated in planned research projects.

a. Power III
b. Secondary data
c. 6-3-5 Brainwriting
d. 180SearchAssistant

Chapter 4. The Human Side of Marketing Research: Organizational and Ethical Issues

1. _____ is an advertisement in which a particular product specifically mentions a competitor by name for the express purpose of showing why the competitor is inferior to the product naming it.

This should not be confused with parody advertisements, where a fictional product is being advertised for the purpose of poking fun at the particular advertisement, nor should it be confused with the use of a coined brand name for the purpose of comparing the product without actually naming an actual competitor. ('Wikipedia tastes better and is less filling than the Encyclopedia Galactica.')

In the 1980s, during what has been referred to as the cola wars, soft-drink manufacturer Pepsi ran a series of advertisements where people, caught on hidden camera, in a blind taste test, chose Pepsi over rival Coca-Cola.

  a. Comparative advertising
  c. GL-70
  b. Cost per conversion
  d. Heavy-up

2. The _____ business model is one in which participants bid for products and services over the Internet. The functionality of buying and selling in an auction format is made possible through auction software which regulates the various processes involved.

Several types of _____s are possible.

  a. ADTECH
  c. ACNielsen
  b. AMAX
  d. Online auction

3. Human beings are also considered to be _____ because they have the ability to change raw materials into valuable _____. The term Human _____ can also be defined as the skills, energies, talents, abilities and knowledge that are used for the production of goods or the rendering of services. While taking into account human beings as _____, the following things have to be kept in mind:

- The size of the population
- The capabilities of the individuals in that population

Many _____ cannot be consumed in their original form. They have to be processed in order to change them into more usable commodities.

  a. Resources
  c. Power III
  b. 6-3-5 Brainwriting
  d. 180SearchAssistant

4. A _____ is a relatively new executive level position at a corporation, company, organization typically reporting directly to the CEO or board of directors. The _____ is responsible for a brand's image, experience, and promise, and propagating it throughout all aspects of the company. The brand officer oversees marketing, advertising, design, public relations and customer service departments.
  a. Chief brand officer
  c. Financial analyst
  b. Chief executive officer
  d. Power III

5. _____ refers to the production of some commodity or service, such as a television program, using a company's own funds, staff, or resources.

Chapter 4. The Human Side of Marketing Research: Organizational and Ethical Issues

This is in contrast to production being outsourced (contracted out) to another company.

- Proprietary

a. In-house
c. ACNielsen
b. Intangible assets
d. Outsourcing

6. A _____ is a collection of symbols, experiences and associations connected with a product, a service, a person or any other artifact or entity.

_____s have become increasingly important components of culture and the economy, now being described as 'cultural accessories and personal philosophies'.

Some people distinguish the psychological aspect of a _____ from the experiential aspect.

a. Brandable software
c. Store brand
b. Brand equity
d. Brand

7. _____ is a measure of the strength of a brand, product, service relative to competitive offerings. There is often a geographic element to the competitive landscape. In defining _____, you must see to what extent a product, brand, or firm controls a product category in a given geographic area.

a. Market system
c. Market dominance
b. Productivity
d. Discretionary spending

8. _____ is defined by the American _____ Association as the activity, set of institutions, and processes for creating, communicating, delivering, and exchanging offerings that have value for customers, clients, partners, and society at large. The term developed from the original meaning which referred literally to going to market, as in shopping, or going to a market to sell goods or services.

_____ practice tends to be seen as a creative industry, which includes advertising, distribution and selling.

a. Marketing myopia
c. Product naming
b. Customer acquisition management
d. Marketing

9. Consumer market research is a form of applied sociology that concentrates on understanding the behaviours, whims and preferences, of consumers in a market-based economy, and aims to understand the effects and comparative success of marketing campaigns. The field of consumer _____ as a statistical science was pioneered by Arthur Nielsen with the founding of the ACNielsen Company in 1923.

Thus _____ is the systematic and objective identification, collection, analysis, and dissemination of information for the purpose of assisting management in decision making related to the identification and solution of problems and opportunities in marketing.

Chapter 4. The Human Side of Marketing Research: Organizational and Ethical Issues

a. Focus group
b. Marketing research process
c. Logit analysis
d. Marketing research

10. _____ generally refers to a list of all planned expenses and revenues. It is a plan for saving and spending. A _____ is an important concept in microeconomics, which uses a _____ line to illustrate the trade-offs between two or more goods.
a. Budget
b. Power III
c. 6-3-5 Brainwriting
d. 180SearchAssistant

11. _____ can be regarded as an outcome of mental processes (cognitive process) leading to the selection of a course of action among several alternatives. Every _____ process produces a final choice. The output can be an action or an opinion of choice.
a. 6-3-5 Brainwriting
b. Power III
c. 180SearchAssistant
d. Decision making

12. In probability theory and statistics, _____ indicates the strength and direction of a linear relationship between two random variables. That is in contrast with the usage of the term in colloquial speech, denoting any relationship, not necessarily linear. In general statistical usage, _____ or co-relation refers to the departure of two random variables from independence.
a. Probability
b. Frequency distribution
c. Mean
d. Correlation

13. A _____ is a group of employees from various functional areas of the organization - research, engineering, marketing, finance. human resources, and operations, for example - who are all focused on a specific objective and are responsible to work as a team to improve coordination and innovation across divisions and resolve mutual problems.
a. Job analysis
b. 180SearchAssistant
c. Power III
d. Cross-functional team

14. _____ is a global marketing research firm, with worldwide headquarters in New York City. Regional headquarters for North America are located in Schaumburg, IL. As of 2008, its the part of The Nielsen Company.
a. InfoNU
b. Alloy Entertainment
c. E-Detailing
d. ACNielsen

15. _____ is a computer program used for statistical analysis.

_____ (originally, Statistical Package for the Social Sciences) was released in its first version in 1968 after being founded by Norman Nie and C. Hadlai Hull. Nie was then a political science postgraduate at Stanford University,and now Research Professor in the Department of Political Science at Stanford and Professor Emeritus of Political Science at the University of Chicago.

a. 180SearchAssistant
b. Power III
c. 6-3-5 Brainwriting
d. SPSS

Chapter 4. The Human Side of Marketing Research: Organizational and Ethical Issues

16. _____ is that part of statistical practice concerned with the selection of individual observations intended to yield some knowledge about a population of concern, especially for the purposes of statistical inference. Each observation measures one or more properties (weight, location, etc.) of an observable entity enumerated to distinguish objects or individuals.
   a. Sampling
   b. Sports Marketing Group
   c. AStore
   d. Richard Buckminster 'Bucky' Fuller

17. A supply chain is the system of organizations, people, technology, activities, information and resources involved in moving a product or service from _____ to customer. Supply chain activities transform natural resources, raw materials and components into a finished product that is delivered to the end customer. In sophisticated supply chain systems, used products may re-enter the supply chain at any point where residual value is recyclable.
   a. Rebate
   b. Product line extension
   c. Bringin' Home the Oil
   d. Supplier

18. A _____ is a psychometric scale commonly used in questionnaires, and is the most widely used scale in survey research. When responding to a Likert questionnaire item, respondents specify their level of agreement to a statement. The scale is named after its inventor, psychologist Rensis Likert.
   a. Likert scale
   b. Factor analysis
   c. Power III
   d. Semantic differential

19. _____ is a mathematical science pertaining to the collection, analysis, interpretation or explanation, and presentation of data. It also provides tools for prediction and forecasting based on data. It is applicable to a wide variety of academic disciplines, from the natural and social sciences to the humanities, government and business.
   a. Median
   b. Type I error
   c. Statistics
   d. Null hypothesis

20. An _____ is a situation that will often involve an apparent conflict between moral imperatives, in which to obey one would result in transgressing another. This is also called an ethical paradox since in moral philosophy, paradox plays a central role in ethics debates. For instance, an ethical admonition to 'love thy neighbour as thy self' is not always just in contrast with, but sometimes in contradiction to an armed neighbour actively trying to kill you: if he or she succeeds, you will not be able to love him or her.
   a. AMAX
   b. Ethical dilemma
   c. ACNielsen
   d. ADTECH

21. _____ is a branch of philosophy which seeks to address questions about morality, such as how a moral outcome can be achieved in a specific situation (applied _____), how moral values should be determined (normative _____), what moral values people actually abide by (descriptive _____), what the fundamental semantic, ontological, and epistemic nature of _____ or morality is (meta-_____), and how moral capacity or moral agency develops and what its nature is (moral psychology.)

Socrates was one of the first Greek philosophers to encourage both scholars and the common citizen to turn their attention from the outside world to the condition of man. In this view, Knowledge having a bearing on human life was placed highest, all other knowledge being secondary.

Chapter 4. The Human Side of Marketing Research: Organizational and Ethical Issues

a. AMAX
b. ACNielsen
c. ADTECH
d. Ethics

22. In statistics, an _____ is a term in a statistical model added when the effect of two or more variables is not simply additive. Such a term reflects that the effect of one variable depends on the values of one or more other variables.

Thus, for a response Y and two variables x_1 and x_2 an additive model would be:

$$Y = ax_1 + bx_2 + \text{error}$$

In contrast to this,

$$Y = ax_1 + bx_2 + c(x_1 \times x_2) + \text{error},$$

is an example of a model with an _____ between variables x_1 and x_2 ('error' refers to the random variable whose value by which y differs from the expected value of y.)

a. ACNielsen
b. ADTECH
c. AMAX
d. Interaction

23. _____ is the area of applied ethics which deals with the moral principles behind the operation and regulation of marketing. Some areas of _____ overlap with media ethics.

Possible frameworks:

- Value-oriented framework, analyzing ethical problems on the basis of the values which they infringe (e.g. honesty, autonomy, privacy, transparency.) An example of such an approach is the AMA Statement of Ethics.
- Stakeholder-oriented framework, analysing ethical problems on the basis of whom they affect (e.g. consumers, competitors, society as a whole.)
- Process-oriented framework, analysing ethical problems in terms of the categories used by marketing specialists (e.g. research, price, promotion, placement.)

None of these frameworks allows, by itself, a convenient and complete categorization of the great variety of issues in _____.

Contrary to popular impressions, not all marketing is adversarial, and not all marketing is stacked in favour of the marketer.

a. 6-3-5 Brainwriting
b. Marketing ethics
c. Power III
d. 180SearchAssistant

Chapter 4. The Human Side of Marketing Research: Organizational and Ethical Issues

24. _____ is a telephone surveying technique in which the interviewer follows a script provided by a software application. The software is able to customize the flow of the questionnaire based on the answers provided, as well as information already known about the participant.

CATI may function in the following manner

- A computerized questionnaire is administered to respondents over the telephone.
- The interviewer sits in front of a computer screen
- Upon command, the computer dials the telephone number to be called.
- When contact is made, the interviewer reads the questions posed on the computer screen and records the respondent's answers directly into the computer.
- Interim and update reports can be compiled instantaneously, as the data are being collected.
- CATI software has built-in logic, which also enhances data accuracy.
- The program will personalize questions and control for logically incorrect answers, such as percentage answers that do not add up to 100 percent.
- The software has built-in branching logic, which will skip questions that are not applicable or will probe for more detail when warranted.

a. 180SearchAssistant
b. Computer-assisted telephone interviewing
c. 6-3-5 Brainwriting
d. Power III

25. _____ has been defined by the International Organization for Standardization (ISO) as 'ensuring that information is accessible only to those authorized to have access' and is one of the cornerstones of information security. _____ is one of the design goals for many cryptosystems, made possible in practice by the techniques of modern cryptography.

_____ also refers to an ethical principle associated with several professions (e.g., medicine, law, religion, professional psychology, and journalism.)

a. Power III
b. 180SearchAssistant
c. 6-3-5 Brainwriting
d. Confidentiality

26. _____ is the ability of an individual or group to seclude themselves or information about themselves and thereby reveal themselves selectively. The boundaries and content of what is considered private differ among cultures and individuals, but share basic common themes. _____ is sometimes related to anonymity, the wish to remain unnoticed or unidentified in the public realm.

a. 180SearchAssistant
b. 6-3-5 Brainwriting
c. Power III
d. Privacy

27. _____ is a method of direct marketing in which a salesperson solicits to prospective customers to buy products or services, either over the phone or through a subsequent face to face or Web conferencing appointment scheduled during the call.

_____ can also include recorded sales pitches programmed to be played over the phone via automatic dialing. _____ has come under fire in recent years, being viewed as an annoyance by many.

Chapter 4. The Human Side of Marketing Research: Organizational and Ethical Issues

a. Joe job
b. Phishing
c. Directory Harvest Attack
d. Telemarketing

28. A number of different _____s are indicated below.

- Randomized controlled trial
    - Double-blind randomized trial
    - Single-blind randomized trial
    - Non-blind trial
- Nonrandomized trial (quasi-experiment)
    - Interrupted time series design (measures on a sample or a series of samples from the same population are obtained several times before and after a manipulated event or a naturally occurring event) - considered a type of quasi-experiment
- Cohort study
    - Prospective cohort
    - Retrospective cohort
    - Time series study
- Case-control study
    - Nested case-control study
- Cross-sectional study
    - Community survey (a type of cross-sectional study)

When choosing a _____, many factors must be taken into account. Different types of studies are subject to different types of bias. For example, recall bias is likely to occur in cross-sectional or case-control studies where subjects are asked to recall exposure to risk factors.

a. 180SearchAssistant
b. Study design
c. Longitudinal studies
d. Power III

29. _____ is computer software that is installed surreptitiously on a personal computer to intercept or take partial control over the user's interaction with the computer, without the user's informed consent.

While the term _____ suggests software that secretly monitors the user's behavior, the functions of _____ extend well beyond simple monitoring. _____ programs can collect various types of personal information, such as Internet surfing habits, sites that have been visited, but can also interfere with user control of the computer in other ways, such as installing additional software, and redirecting Web browser activity.

a. 6-3-5 Brainwriting
b. 180SearchAssistant
c. Power III
d. Spyware

30. A _____ is any statistical test for which the distribution of the test statistic under the null hypothesis can be approximated by a normal distribution. Since many test statistics are approximately normally distributed for large samples (due to the central limit theorem), many statistical tests can be performed as approximate _____s if the sample size is not too small. In addition, some statistical tests such as comparisons of means between two samples, or a comparison of the mean of one sample to a given constant, are exact _____s under certain assumptions.

a. Sample size
b. Confounding variables
c. Null hypothesis
d. Z-test

31. _____ describes data and characteristics about the population or phenomenon being studied. _____ answers the questions who, what, where, when and how.

Although the data description is factual, accurate and systematic, the research cannot describe what caused a situation.

a. Power III
b. Two-tailed test
c. Sampling error
d. Descriptive research

32. Mystery shopping or Mystery Consumer is a tool used by market research companies to measure quality of retail service or gather specific information about products and services. _____ posing as normal customers perform specific tasks-- such as purchasing a product, asking questions, registering complaints or behaving in a certain way - and then provide detailed reports or feedback about their experiences.

Mystery shopping began in the 1940s as a way to measure employee integrity.

a. Mystery shopping
b. Market research
c. Questionnaire
d. Mystery shoppers

33. The _____ is an independent agency of the United States government, established in 1914 by the _____ Act. Its principal mission is the promotion of 'consumer protection' and the elimination and prevention of what regulators perceive to be harmfully 'anti-competitive' business practices, such as coercive monopoly.

The _____ Act was one of President Wilson's major acts against trusts.

a. Power III
b. Federal Trade Commission
c. 6-3-5 Brainwriting
d. 180SearchAssistant

34. _____ is a form of applied ethics that examines ethical principles and moral or ethical problems that arise in a business environment. It applies to all aspects of business conduct and is relevant to the conduct of individuals and business organizations as a whole. Applied ethics is a field of ethics that deals with ethical questions in many fields such as medical, technical, legal and _____.

a. 6-3-5 Brainwriting
b. Business ethics
c. Power III
d. 180SearchAssistant

35. The _____ is a professional association for marketers. As of 2008 it had approximately 40,000 members. There are collegiate chapters on 250 campuses.

a. ADTECH
b. ACNielsen
c. AMAX
d. American Marketing Association

36. The business terms _____ and pull originated in the logistic and supply chain management, but are also widely used in marketing.

Chapter 4. The Human Side of Marketing Research: Organizational and Ethical Issues

A _____-pull-system in business describes the move of a product or information between two subjects. On markets the consumers usually 'pulls' the goods or information they demand for their needs, while the offerers or suppliers '_____es' them toward the consumers.

   a. Manufacturers' representatives
   b. Gold Key Matching Service
   c. Push
   d. Completely randomized designs

37. A _____ is a political campaign technique in which an individual or organization attempts to influence or alter the view of respondents under the guise of conducting a poll. In a _____, large numbers of respondents are contacted, and little or no effort is made to collect and analyze response data. Instead, the _____ is a form of telemarketing-based propaganda and rumor mongering, masquerading as a poll.
   a. Power III
   b. 180SearchAssistant
   c. 6-3-5 Brainwriting
   d. Push poll

38. _____ is a fee paid on borrowed assets. It is the price paid for the use of borrowed money, or, money earned by deposited funds. Assets that are sometimes lent with _____ include money, shares, consumer goods through hire purchase, major assets such as aircraft, and even entire factories in finance lease arrangements.
   a. ACNielsen
   b. AMAX
   c. Interest
   d. ADTECH

39. _____ is the pursuit of influencing outcomes -- including public-policy and resource allocation decisions within political, economic, and social systems and institutions -- that directly affect people's current lives. (Cohen, 2001)

Therefore, _____ can be seen as a deliberate process of speaking out on issues of concern in order to exert some influence on behalf of ideas or persons. Based on this definition, Cohen (2001) states that 'ideologues of all persuasions advocate' to bring a change in people's lives.

   a. Advocacy
   b. ADTECH
   c. ACNielsen
   d. AMAX

40. Procter is a surname, and may also refer to:

   - Bryan Waller Procter (pseud. Barry Cornwall), English poet
   - Goodwin Procter, American law firm
   - _____, consumer products multinational

   a. Flyer
   b. Procter ' Gamble
   c. Convergent
   d. Black PRies

41. The _____ is a global navigation satellite system (GNSS) developed by the United States Department of Defense and managed by the United States Air Force 50th Space Wing. It is the only fully functional GNSS in the world, can be used freely, and is often used by civilians for navigation purposes. It uses a constellation of between 24 and 32 Medium Earth Orbit satellites that transmit precise microwave signals, which allow _____ receivers to determine their current location, the time, and their velocity.

a. Global positioning system
b. Power III
c. 180SearchAssistant
d. 6-3-5 Brainwriting

Chapter 5. Problem Definition: Jump-Starting the Research Process

1. _____ refer to a collection of facts usually collected as the result of experience, observation or experiment or a set of premises. This may consist of numbers, words particularly as measurements or observations of a set of variables. _____ are often viewed as a lowest level of abstraction from which information and knowledge are derived.
    a. Sample size
    b. Pearson product-moment correlation coefficient
    c. Mean
    d. Data

2. _____ can be regarded as an outcome of mental processes (cognitive process) leading to the selection of a course of action among several alternatives. Every _____ process produces a final choice. The output can be an action or an opinion of choice.
    a. 180SearchAssistant
    b. Power III
    c. Decision making
    d. 6-3-5 Brainwriting

3. _____ is that part of statistical practice concerned with the selection of individual observations intended to yield some knowledge about a population of concern, especially for the purposes of statistical inference. Each observation measures one or more properties (weight, location, etc.) of an observable entity enumerated to distinguish objects or individuals.
    a. Sampling
    b. AStore
    c. Richard Buckminster 'Bucky' Fuller
    d. Sports Marketing Group

4. _____ is a marketing term, and involves evaluating the situation and trends in a particular company's market. _____ is often called the 'three c's', which refers to the three major elements that must be studied:

- Customers
- Costs
- Competition

The number of 'c's' is sometimes extended to four, five, or even six, with 'Collaboration', 'Company', and 'Competitive advantage'.

- Marketing mix
- SWOT analysis

    a. Power III
    b. 6-3-5 Brainwriting
    c. Situation analysis
    d. 180SearchAssistant

5. _____ is an advertisement in which a particular product specifically mentions a competitor by name for the express purpose of showing why the competitor is inferior to the product naming it.

This should not be confused with parody advertisements, where a fictional product is being advertised for the purpose of poking fun at the particular advertisement, nor should it be confused with the use of a coined brand name for the purpose of comparing the product without actually naming an actual competitor. ('Wikipedia tastes better and is less filling than the Encyclopedia Galactica.')

In the 1980s, during what has been referred to as the cola wars, soft-drink manufacturer Pepsi ran a series of advertisements where people, caught on hidden camera, in a blind taste test, chose Pepsi over rival Coca-Cola.

Chapter 5. Problem Definition: Jump-Starting the Research Process

   a. Cost per conversion   b. GL-70
   c. Heavy-up   d. Comparative advertising

6. The _____ is the major entity that is being analyzed in the study. It is the 'what' or 'whom' that is being studied. In social science research, the most typical units of analysis are individual people.
   a. ACNielsen   b. ADTECH
   c. AMAX   d. Unit of analysis

7. _____ is a broad label that refers to any individuals or households that use goods and services generated within the economy. The concept of a _____ is used in different contexts, so that the usage and significance of the term may vary.

A _____ is a person who uses any product or service.

   a. Power III   b. 6-3-5 Brainwriting
   c. 180SearchAssistant   d. Consumer

8. A personal and cultural _____ is a relative ethic _____, an assumption upon which implementation can be extrapolated. A _____ system is a set of consistent _____s and measures that is soo not true. A principle _____ is a foundation upon which other _____s and measures of integrity are based.
   a. Supreme Court of the United States   b. Value
   c. Perceptual maps   d. Package-on-Package

9. _____ is a telephone surveying technique in which the interviewer follows a script provided by a software application. The software is able to customize the flow of the questionnaire based on the answers provided, as well as information already known about the participant.

CATI may function in the following manner

- A computerized questionnaire is administered to respondents over the telephone.
- The interviewer sits in front of a computer screen
- Upon command, the computer dials the telephone number to be called.
- When contact is made, the interviewer reads the questions posed on the computer screen and records the respondent's answers directly into the computer.
- Interim and update reports can be compiled instantaneously, as the data are being collected.
- CATI software has built-in logic, which also enhances data accuracy.
- The program will personalize questions and control for logically incorrect answers, such as percentage answers that do not add up to 100 percent.
- The software has built-in branching logic, which will skip questions that are not applicable or will probe for more detail when warranted.

   a. Power III   b. 6-3-5 Brainwriting
   c. Computer-assisted telephone interviewing   d. 180SearchAssistant

Chapter 5. Problem Definition: Jump-Starting the Research Process

10. The terms '_____' and 'independent variable' are used in similar but subtly different ways in mathematics and statistics as part of the standard terminology in those subjects. They are used to distinguish between two types of quantities being considered, separating them into those available at the start of a process and those being created by it, where the latter (_____s) are dependent on the former (independent variables.)

In traditional calculus, a function is defined as a relation between two terms called variables because their values vary.

   a. Dependent variable
   b. Field experiment
   c. 180SearchAssistant
   d. Power III

11. _____s are used in open sentences. For instance, in the formula x + 1 = 5, x is a _____ which represents an 'unknown' number. _____s are often represented by letters of the Roman alphabet, or those of other alphabets, such as Greek, and use other special symbols.
   a. Personalization
   b. Book of business
   c. Quantitative
   d. Variable

12. _____ is defined by the American _____ Association as the activity, set of institutions, and processes for creating, communicating, delivering, and exchanging offerings that have value for customers, clients, partners, and society at large. The term developed from the original meaning which referred literally to going to market, as in shopping, or going to a market to sell goods or services.

_____ practice tends to be seen as a creative industry, which includes advertising, distribution and selling.

   a. Marketing
   b. Customer acquisition management
   c. Marketing myopia
   d. Product naming

13. Consumer market research is a form of applied sociology that concentrates on understanding the behaviours, whims and preferences, of consumers in a market-based economy, and aims to understand the effects and comparative success of marketing campaigns. The field of consumer _____ as a statistical science was pioneered by Arthur Nielsen with the founding of the ACNielsen Company in 1923.

Thus _____ is the systematic and objective identification, collection, analysis, and dissemination of information for the purpose of assisting management in decision making related to the identification and solution of problems and opportunities in marketing.

   a. Logit analysis
   b. Marketing research
   c. Marketing research process
   d. Focus group

14. A _____ is any statistical test for which the distribution of the test statistic under the null hypothesis can be approximated by a normal distribution. Since many test statistics are approximately normally distributed for large samples (due to the central limit theorem), many statistical tests can be performed as approximate _____s if the sample size is not too small. In addition, some statistical tests such as comparisons of means between two samples, or a comparison of the mean of one sample to a given constant, are exact _____s under certain assumptions.

Chapter 5. Problem Definition: Jump-Starting the Research Process

a. Confounding variables
c. Null hypothesis
b. Sample size
d. Z-test

15. In probability theory and statistics, _____ indicates the strength and direction of a linear relationship between two random variables. That is in contrast with the usage of the term in colloquial speech, denoting any relationship, not necessarily linear. In general statistical usage, _____ or co-relation refers to the departure of two random variables from independence.

a. Frequency distribution
c. Mean
b. Probability
d. Correlation

16. _____ is a business discipline which is focused on the practical application of marketing techniques and the management of a firm's marketing resources and activities. Marketing managers are often responsible for influencing the level, timing, and composition of customer demand accepted definition of the term. In part, this is because the role of a marketing manager can vary significantly based on a business' size, corporate culture, and industry context.

a. Door-to-door
c. Performance-based advertising
b. Business structure
d. Marketing Management

Chapter 6. Qualitative Research Tools

1. A _____ attribute is one that exists in a range of magnitudes, and can therefore be measured. Measurements of any particular _____ property are expressed as a specific quantity, referred to as a unit, multiplied by a number. Examples of physical quantities are distance, mass, and time.
   a. Dolly Dimples
   b. Lifestyle city
   c. BeyondROI
   d. Quantitative

2. Procter is a surname, and may also refer to:

   - Bryan Waller Procter (pseud. Barry Cornwall), English poet
   - Goodwin Procter, American law firm
   - _____, consumer products multinational

   a. Convergent
   b. Black PRies
   c. Flyer
   d. Procter ' Gamble

3. _____ is that part of statistical practice concerned with the selection of individual observations intended to yield some knowledge about a population of concern, especially for the purposes of statistical inference. Each observation measures one or more properties (weight, location, etc.) of an observable entity enumerated to distinguish objects or individuals.
   a. Sampling
   b. AStore
   c. Sports Marketing Group
   d. Richard Buckminster 'Bucky' Fuller

4. _____ is a type of research conducted because a problem has not been clearly defined. _____ helps determine the best research design, data collection method and selection of subjects. Given its fundamental nature, _____ often concludes that a perceived problem does not actually exist.
   a. IDDEA
   b. Intent scale translation
   c. ACNielsen
   d. Exploratory research

5. _____ is a field of inquiry that crosscuts disciplines and subject matters . _____ers aim to gather an in-depth understanding of human behavior and the reasons that govern such behavior. The discipline investigates the why and how of decision making, not just what, where, when.
   a. 6-3-5 Brainwriting
   b. 180SearchAssistant
   c. Power III
   d. Qualitative research

6. _____ is an advertisement in which a particular product specifically mentions a competitor by name for the express purpose of showing why the competitor is inferior to the product naming it.

This should not be confused with parody advertisements, where a fictional product is being advertised for the purpose of poking fun at the particular advertisement, nor should it be confused with the use of a coined brand name for the purpose of comparing the product without actually naming an actual competitor. ('Wikipedia tastes better and is less filling than the Encyclopedia Galactica.')

In the 1980s, during what has been referred to as the cola wars, soft-drink manufacturer Pepsi ran a series of advertisements where people, caught on hidden camera, in a blind taste test, chose Pepsi over rival Coca-Cola.

Chapter 6. Qualitative Research Tools

a. Comparative advertising
b. GL-70
c. Heavy-up
d. Cost per conversion

7. _____ is a telephone surveying technique in which the interviewer follows a script provided by a software application. The software is able to customize the flow of the questionnaire based on the answers provided, as well as information already known about the participant.

CATI may function in the following manner

- A computerized questionnaire is administered to respondents over the telephone.
- The interviewer sits in front of a computer screen
- Upon command, the computer dials the telephone number to be called.
- When contact is made, the interviewer reads the questions posed on the computer screen and records the respondent's answers directly into the computer.
- Interim and update reports can be compiled instantaneously, as the data are being collected.
- CATI software has built-in logic, which also enhances data accuracy.
- The program will personalize questions and control for logically incorrect answers, such as percentage answers that do not add up to 100 percent.
- The software has built-in branching logic, which will skip questions that are not applicable or will probe for more detail when warranted.

a. 6-3-5 Brainwriting
b. 180SearchAssistant
c. Power III
d. Computer-assisted telephone interviewing

8. _____ is the process of using quantitative methods and qualitative methods to evaluate consumer response to a product idea prior to the introduction of a product to the market. It can also be used to generate communication designed to alter consumer attitudes toward existing products. These methods involve the evaluation by consumers of product concepts having certain rational benefits, such as 'a detergent that removes stains but is gentle on fabrics,' or non-rational benefits, such as 'a shampoo that lets you be yourself.' Such methods are commonly referred to as _____ and have been performed using field surveys, personal interviews and focus groups, in combination with various quantitative methods, to generate and evaluate product concepts.

a. Logit analysis
b. Cross tabulation
c. Market analysis
d. Concept testing

9. _____ refer to a collection of facts usually collected as the result of experience, observation or experiment or a set of premises. This may consist of numbers, words particularly as measurements or observations of a set of variables. _____ are often viewed as a lowest level of abstraction from which information and knowledge are derived.

a. Pearson product-moment correlation coefficient
b. Mean
c. Sample size
d. Data

10. In probability theory and statistics, _____ indicates the strength and direction of a linear relationship between two random variables. That is in contrast with the usage of the term in colloquial speech, denoting any relationship, not necessarily linear. In general statistical usage, _____ or co-relation refers to the departure of two random variables from independence.

Chapter 6. Qualitative Research Tools

a. Probability
b. Correlation
c. Mean
d. Frequency distribution

11. _____ is a genre of writing that uses fieldwork to provide a descriptive study of human societies. _____ presents the results of a holistic research method founded on the idea that a system's properties cannot necessarily be accurately understood independently of each other. The genre has both formal and historical connections to travel writing and colonial office reports.
    a. ADTECH
    b. Ethnography
    c. ACNielsen
    d. AMAX

12. The _____ is a global navigation satellite system (GNSS) developed by the United States Department of Defense and managed by the United States Air Force 50th Space Wing. It is the only fully functional GNSS in the world, can be used freely, and is often used by civilians for navigation purposes. It uses a constellation of between 24 and 32 Medium Earth Orbit satellites that transmit precise microwave signals, which allow _____ receivers to determine their current location, the time, and their velocity.
    a. Power III
    b. 180SearchAssistant
    c. 6-3-5 Brainwriting
    d. Global positioning system

13. A personal and cultural _____ is a relative ethic _____, an assumption upon which implementation can be extrapolated. A _____ system is a set of consistent _____s and measures that is soo not true. A principle _____ is a foundation upon which other _____s and measures of integrity are based.
    a. Supreme Court of the United States
    b. Perceptual maps
    c. Package-on-Package
    d. Value

14. A _____ is a form of qualitative research in which a group of people are asked about their attitude towards a product, service, concept, advertisement, idea, or packaging. Questions are asked in an interactive group setting where participants are free to talk with other group members.

Ernest Dichter originated the idea of having a 'group therapy' for products and this process is what became known as a _____.

    a. Focus group
    b. Cross tabulation
    c. Logit analysis
    d. Marketing research process

15. _____ is a measure of the strength of a brand, product, service relative to competitive offerings. There is often a geographic element to the competitive landscape. In defining _____, you must see to what extent a product, brand, or firm controls a product category in a given geographic area.
    a. Productivity
    b. Market dominance
    c. Discretionary spending
    d. Market system

16. A _____ is a type of website, usually maintained by an individual with regular entries of commentary, descriptions of events, or other material such as graphics or video. Entries are commonly displayed in reverse-chronological order. '_____' can also be used as a verb, meaning to maintain or add content to a _____.
    a. 180SearchAssistant
    b. Blog
    c. Power III
    d. 6-3-5 Brainwriting

Chapter 6. Qualitative Research Tools

17. An _____ is one type of focus group, and is a sub-set of online research methods.

A moderator invites prescreened, qualified respondents who represent the target of interest to log on to conferencing software at a pre-arranged time and to take part in an _____. Some researchers will offer incentives for participating but this raises a number of ethical questions.

   a. Automated surveys
   c. Intangibility
   b. Engagement
   d. Online focus group

18. _____ is multimedia that is constantly received by, and normally presented to, an end-user while it is being delivered by a streaming provider (the term 'presented' is used in this article in a general sense that includes audio or video playback.) The name refers to the delivery method of the medium rather than to the medium itself. The distinction is usually applied to media that are distributed over telecommunications networks, as most other delivery systems are either inherently streaming (e.g. radio, television) or inherently non-streaming (e.g. books, video cassettes, audio CDs.)
   a. Power III
   c. 6-3-5 Brainwriting
   b. 180SearchAssistant
   d. Streaming media

19. _____ is an investment technique that requires investors to purchase multiple financial products with different maturity dates.

_____ avoids the risk of reinvesting a big portion of assets in an unfavorable financial environment. For example, a person has both a 2015 matured CD and a 2018 matured CD.

   a. 180SearchAssistant
   c. 6-3-5 Brainwriting
   b. Laddering
   d. Power III

20. _____ is a broad label that refers to any individuals or households that use goods and services generated within the economy. The concept of a _____ is used in different contexts, so that the usage and significance of the term may vary.

A _____ is a person who uses any product or service.

   a. Power III
   c. 6-3-5 Brainwriting
   b. 180SearchAssistant
   d. Consumer

21. The _____ is an example of a projective test.

Historically, the _____ or _____ has been amongst the most widely used, researched, and taught projective psychological tests. Its adherents claim that it taps a subject's unconscious to reveal repressed aspects of personality, motives and needs for achievement, power and intimacy, and problem-solving abilities.

   a. Power III
   c. 180SearchAssistant
   b. Thematic apperception test
   d. 6-3-5 Brainwriting

22. _____ can be regarded as an outcome of mental processes (cognitive process) leading to the selection of a course of action among several alternatives. Every _____ process produces a final choice. The output can be an action or an opinion of choice.

    a. Power III
    b. 6-3-5 Brainwriting
    c. Decision making
    d. 180SearchAssistant

23. _____ generally refers to a list of all planned expenses and revenues. It is a plan for saving and spending. A _____ is an important concept in microeconomics, which uses a _____ line to illustrate the trade-offs between two or more goods.

    a. 180SearchAssistant
    b. 6-3-5 Brainwriting
    c. Power III
    d. Budget

Chapter 7. Secondary Data Research in a Digital Age

1. _____ is a form of communication that typically attempts to persuade potential customers to purchase or to consume more of a particular brand of product or service. 'While now central to the contemporary global economy and the reproduction of global production networks, it is only quite recently that _____ has been more than a marginal influence on patterns of sales and production. The formation of modern _____ was intimately bound up with the emergence of new forms of monopoly capitalism around the end of the 19th and beginning of the 20th century as one element in corporate strategies to create, organize and where possible control markets, especially for mass produced consumer goods.
    a. Advertising
    b. ADTECH
    c. ACNielsen
    d. AMAX

2. _____ often refers to either primary or secondary research. Secondary research involves a company using information compiled from various sources, which is about a new or existing product. The advantages of secondary research are that it is relatively cheap and easily accessible.
    a. Mystery shoppers
    b. Mystery shopping
    c. Questionnaire
    d. Market Research

3. _____ refer to a collection of facts usually collected as the result of experience, observation or experiment or a set of premises. This may consist of numbers, words particularly as measurements or observations of a set of variables. _____ are often viewed as a lowest level of abstraction from which information and knowledge are derived.
    a. Mean
    b. Pearson product-moment correlation coefficient
    c. Sample size
    d. Data

4. _____ is a mathematical science pertaining to the collection, analysis, interpretation or explanation, and presentation of data. It also provides tools for prediction and forecasting based on data. It is applicable to a wide variety of academic disciplines, from the natural and social sciences to the humanities, government and business.
    a. Statistics
    b. Median
    c. Type I error
    d. Null hypothesis

5. _____ is a process of gathering, analyzing, and dispensing information for tactical or strategic purposes. The _____ process entails obtaining both factual and subjective information on the business environments in which a company is operating or considering entering.

There are three ways of scanning the business environment:

- Ad-hoc scanning - Short term, infrequent examinations usually initiated by a crisis
- Regular scanning - Studies done on a regular schedule (say, once a year)
- Continuous scanning(also called continuous learning) - continuous structured data collection and processing on a broad range of environmental factors

Most commentators feel that in today's turbulent business environment the best scanning method available is continuous scanning.This allows the firm to :

-act quickly-take advantage of opportunities before competitors do-respond to environmental threats before significant damage is done

The Macro Environment

_____ usually refers just to the macro environment, but it can also include:-industry -competitor analysis -marketing research(consumer analysis) -New Product Development(product innovations)- the company's internal environment

Macro _____ involves analysing:

- The Economy

GDP per capitaeconomic growthunemployment]] rateinflation]] rateconsumer and investor confidenceinventory levelscurrency exchange ratesmerchandise trade balancefinancial and political health of trading partnersbalance of paymentsfuture trends

- Government

political climate - amount of government activitypolitical stability and riskgovernment debtbudget deficit or surpluscorporate and personal tax ratespayroll taxesimport tariffs and quotasexport restrictionsrestrictions on international financial flows

- Legal

minimum wage lawsenvironmental protection lawsworker safety lawsunion lawscopyright and patent lawsanti- monopoly lawsSunday closing lawsmunicipal licenceslaws that favour business investment

- Technology

efficiency of infrastructure, including: roads, ports, airports, rolling stock, hospitals, education, healthcare, communication, etc.industrial productivitynew manufacturing processesnew products and services of competitorsnew products and services of supply chain partnersany new technology that could impact the companycost and accessibility of electrical power

- Ecology
  - ecological concerns that affect the firms production processes
  - ecological concerns that affect customers' buying habits
  - ecological concerns that affect customers' perception of the company or product
- Socio-Cultural
  - demographic factors such as:
    - population size and distribution
    - age distribution
    - education levels
    - income levels
    - ethnic origins
    - religious affiliations
  - attitudes towards:
    - materialism, capitalism, free enterprise
    - individualism, role of family, role of government, collectivism
    - role of church and religion
    - consumerism
    - environmentalism
    - importance of work, pride of accomplishment
  - cultural structures including:
    - diet and nutrition
    - housing conditions
- Potential Suppliers
  - Labour supply
    - quantity of labour available
    - quality of labour available
    - stability of labour supply
    - wage expectations
    - employee turn-over rate
    - strikes and labour relations
    - educational facilities
  - Material suppliers
    - quality, quantity, price, and stability of material inputs
    - delivery delays
    - proximity of bulky or heavy material inputs
    - level of competition among suppliers
  - Service Providers
    - quantity, quality, price, and stability of service facilitators
    - special requirements
- Stakeholders
  - Lobbyists
  - Shareholders
  - Employees
  - Partners

Chapter 7. Secondary Data Research in a Digital Age

Scanning these macro environmental variables for threats and opportunities requires that each issue be rated on two dimensions. It must be rated on its potential impact on the company, and rated on its likeliness of occurrence.

a. Environmental scanning
b. ADTECH
c. ACNielsen
d. AMAX

6. _____ is the process of extracting hidden patterns from data. As more data is gathered, with the amount of data doubling every three years, _____ is becoming an increasingly important tool to transform this data into information. It is commonly used in a wide range of profiling practices, such as marketing, surveillance, fraud detection and scientific discovery.

a. Structure mining
b. 180SearchAssistant
c. Power III
d. Data mining

7. Traditionally, the term _____ had been used to refer to a network or circuit of biological neurons. The modern usage of the term often refers to artificial _____s, which are composed of artificial neurons or nodes. Thus the term has two distinct usages:

1. Biological _____s are made up of real biological neurons that are connected or functionally related in the peripheral nervous system or the central nervous system. In the field of neuroscience, they are often identified as groups of neurons that perform a specific physiological function in laboratory analysis.
2. Artificial _____s are made up of interconnecting artificial neurons (programming constructs that mimic the properties of biological neurons.) Artificial _____s may either be used to gain an understanding of biological _____s, or for solving artificial intelligence problems without necessarily creating a model of a real biological system. The real, biological nervous system is highly complex and includes some features that may seem superfluous based on an understanding of artificial networks

In general a biological _____ is composed of a group or groups of chemically connected or functionally associated neurons.

a. Power III
b. 180SearchAssistant
c. Neural network
d. 6-3-5 Brainwriting

8. A _____ is a type of website, usually maintained by an individual with regular entries of commentary, descriptions of events, or other material such as graphics or video. Entries are commonly displayed in reverse-chronological order. '_____' can also be used as a verb, meaning to maintain or add content to a _____.

a. Power III
b. 180SearchAssistant
c. 6-3-5 Brainwriting
d. Blog

9. _____ consists of the processes a company uses to track and organize its contacts with its current and prospective customers. _____ software is used to support these processes; information about customers and customer interactions can be entered, stored and accessed by employees in different company departments. Typical _____ goals are to improve services provided to customers, and to use customer contact information for targeted marketing.

Chapter 7. Secondary Data Research in a Digital Age

a. Product bundling
c. Demand generation
b. Commercialization
d. Customer relationship management

10. A _____ is a structured collection of records or data that is stored in a computer system. The structure is achieved by organizing the data according to a _____ model. The model in most common use today is the relational model.
a. 6-3-5 Brainwriting
c. Power III
b. Database
d. 180SearchAssistant

11. _____ is a form of direct marketing using databases of customers or potential customers to generate personalized communications in order to promote a product or service for marketing purposes. The method of communication can be any addressable medium, as in direct marketing.

The distinction between direct and _____ stems primarily from the attention paid to the analysis of data.

a. Direct Marketing Associations
c. Power III
b. Database marketing
d. Direct marketing

12. _____ is defined by the American _____ Association as the activity, set of institutions, and processes for creating, communicating, delivering, and exchanging offerings that have value for customers, clients, partners, and society at large. The term developed from the original meaning which referred literally to going to market, as in shopping, or going to a market to sell goods or services.

_____ practice tends to be seen as a creative industry, which includes advertising, distribution and selling.

a. Product naming
c. Marketing myopia
b. Marketing
d. Customer acquisition management

13. Customer _____ consists of the processes a company uses to track and organize its contacts with its current and prospective customers. CRelationship management software is used to support these processes; information about customers and customer interactions can be entered, stored and accessed by employees in different company departments. Typical CRelationship management goals are to improve services provided to customers, and to use customer contact information for targeted marketing.
a. Product bundling
c. Marketing
b. Green marketing
d. Relationship management

14. Combining Existing _____ Sources with New Primary Data Sources

Imagine that we could get hold of a good collection of surveys taken in earlier years, such as detailed studies about changes going on in this phase and hopefully additional studies in the years to come. Analyzing this data base over time could give us a good picture of what changes actually have taken place in the orientation of the population and of the extent to which new technical concepts did have an impact on subgroups of the population. Furthermore, data archives can help to prepare studies on change over time by monitoring what questions have been asked in earlier years and alerting principal investigators to important questions which should be repeated in planned research projects.

a. 180SearchAssistant
b. Power III
c. 6-3-5 Brainwriting
d. Secondary data

15. Human beings are also considered to be _____ because they have the ability to change raw materials into valuable _____. The term Human _____ can also be defined as the skills, energies, talents, abilities and knowledge that are used for the production of goods or the rendering of services. While taking into account human beings as _____, the following things have to be kept in mind:

- The size of the population
- The capabilities of the individuals in that population

Many _____ cannot be consumed in their original form. They have to be processed in order to change them into more usable commodities.

a. Power III
b. 180SearchAssistant
c. 6-3-5 Brainwriting
d. Resources

16. _____ is that part of statistical practice concerned with the selection of individual observations intended to yield some knowledge about a population of concern, especially for the purposes of statistical inference. Each observation measures one or more properties (weight, location, etc.) of an observable entity enumerated to distinguish objects or individuals.

a. Richard Buckminster 'Bucky' Fuller
b. AStore
c. Sports Marketing Group
d. Sampling

17. _____ is one of the four elements of marketing mix. An organization or set of organizations (go-betweens) involved in the process of making a product or service available for use or consumption by a consumer or business user.

The other three parts of the marketing mix are product, pricing, and promotion.

a. Japan Advertising Photographers' Association
b. Comparison-Shopping agent
c. Better Living Through Chemistry
d. Distribution

18. In economics, an externality or spillover of an economic transaction is an impact on a party that is not directly involved in the transaction. In such a case, prices do not reflect the full costs or benefits in production or consumption of a product or service. A positive impact is called an _____ benefit, while a negative impact is called an _____ cost.

a. AMAX
b. ACNielsen
c. ADTECH
d. External

19. Many institutions make a distinction between circulating _____ and collecting _____ Many modern _____ are a mixture of both, as they contain a general collection for circulation, and a reference collection which is often more specialized, as well as restricted to the library premises.

Also, the governments of most major countries support national _____.

a. 180SearchAssistant	b. 6-3-5 Brainwriting
c. Power III	d. Libraries

20. Procter is a surname, and may also refer to:

- Bryan Waller Procter (pseud. Barry Cornwall), English poet
- Goodwin Procter, American law firm
- _____, consumer products multinational

a. Flyer	b. Convergent
c. Black PRies	d. Procter ' Gamble

21. _____ is a global marketing research firm, with worldwide headquarters in New York City. Regional headquarters for North America are located in Schaumburg, IL. As of 2008, its the part of The Nielsen Company.

a. InfoNU	b. E-Detailing
c. Alloy Entertainment	d. ACNielsen

22. _____ in economics and business is the result of an exchange and from that trade we assign a numerical monetary value to a good, service or asset. If I trade 4 apples for an orange, the _____ of an orange is 4 - apples. Inversely, the _____ of an apple is 1/4 oranges.

a. Price	b. Discounts and allowances
c. Contribution margin-based pricing	d. Pricing

Chapter 8. Survey Research: An Overview

1. _____ a research method involving the use of questionnaires and/or statistical surveys to gather data about people and their thoughts and behaviours.
   a. T-test
   b. Control chart
   c. Z-test
   d. Survey research

2. _____ is that part of statistical practice concerned with the selection of individual observations intended to yield some knowledge about a population of concern, especially for the purposes of statistical inference. Each observation measures one or more properties (weight, location, etc.) of an observable entity enumerated to distinguish objects or individuals.
   a. AStore
   b. Sampling
   c. Richard Buckminster 'Bucky' Fuller
   d. Sports Marketing Group

3. _____ is a standard point of view or personal prejudice. especially when the tendency interferes with the ability to be impartial, unprejudiced, or objective. The term _____ed is used to describe an action, judgment, or other outcome influenced by a prejudged perspective.
   a. Bias
   b. Power III
   c. 6-3-5 Brainwriting
   d. 180SearchAssistant

4. _____s are biases in measurement which lead to the situation where the mean of many separate measurements differs significantly from the actual value of the measured attribute. All measurements are prone to _____s, often of several different types. Sources of _____ may be imperfect calibration of measurement instruments, changes in the environment which interfere with the measurement process and sometimes imperfect methods of observation can be either zero error or percentage error.
   a. 180SearchAssistant
   b. Systematic bias
   c. Power III
   d. Systematic error

5. _____, a business term, is a measure of how products and services supplied by a company meet or surpass customer expectation. It is seen as a key performance indicator within business and is part of the four perspectives of a Balanced Scorecard.

   In a competitive marketplace where businesses compete for customers, _____ is seen as a key differentiator and increasingly has become a key element of business strategy.

   a. Customer satisfaction
   b. Psychological pricing
   c. Customer base
   d. Supplier diversity

6. _____ is a type of cognitive bias which can affect the results of a statistical survey if respondents answer questions in the way they think the questioner wants them to answer rather than according to their true beliefs. This may occur if the questioner is obviously angling for a particular answer (as in push polling) or if the respondent wishes to please the questioner by answering what appears to be the 'morally right' answer. An example of the latter might be if a woman surveys a man on his attitudes to domestic violence, or someone who obviously cares about the environment asks people how much they value a wilderness area.
   a. 180SearchAssistant
   b. Von Restorff effect
   c. Response bias
   d. Power III

Chapter 8. Survey Research: An Overview

7. A _____ is any statistical test for which the distribution of the test statistic under the null hypothesis can be approximated by a normal distribution. Since many test statistics are approximately normally distributed for large samples (due to the central limit theorem), many statistical tests can be performed as approximate _____s if the sample size is not too small. In addition, some statistical tests such as comparisons of means between two samples, or a comparison of the mean of one sample to a given constant, are exact _____s under certain assumptions.
   a. Null hypothesis
   b. Z-test
   c. Confounding variables
   d. Sample size

8. _____ is a category of response bias in which respondents to a survey have a tendency to agree with all the questions or to indicate a positive connotation.
   a. ACNielsen
   b. ADTECH
   c. AMAX
   d. Acquiescence bias

9. _____ refer to a collection of facts usually collected as the result of experience, observation or experiment or a set of premises. This may consist of numbers, words particularly as measurements or observations of a set of variables. _____ are often viewed as a lowest level of abstraction from which information and knowledge are derived.
   a. Mean
   b. Sample size
   c. Pearson product-moment correlation coefficient
   d. Data

10. A _____ is an error that occurs when a person performs an action on an object that is not the object intended. This error can be very disorienting and usually causes a brief loss of situation awareness or automation surprise if noticed right away. But much worse, if it goes unnoticed, it could cause more serious problems.
    a. 180SearchAssistant
    b. Motivation
    c. Power III
    d. Description error

11. _____ form a class of research methods that involve observation of some subset of a population of items all at the same time, in which, groups can be compared at different ages with respect of independent variables, such as IQ and memory. The fundamental difference between cross-sectional and longitudinal studies is that _____ take place at a single point in time and that a longitudinal study involves a series of measurements taken over a period of time. Both are a type of observational study.
    a. 180SearchAssistant
    b. Cross-sectional studies
    c. Longitudinal studies
    d. Power III

12. _____ is a measure of the strength of a brand, product, service relative to competitive offerings. There is often a geographic element to the competitive landscape. In defining _____, you must see to what extent a product, brand, or firm controls a product category in a given geographic area.
    a. Market system
    b. Discretionary spending
    c. Productivity
    d. Market dominance

13. A longitudinal study is a correlational research study that involves repeated observations of the same items over long periods of time -- often many decades. It is a type of observational study. _____ are often used in psychology to study developmental trends across the life span.
    a. 180SearchAssistant
    b. Power III
    c. Longitudinal studies
    d. Study design

Chapter 8. Survey Research: An Overview

14. _____ is an advertisement in which a particular product specifically mentions a competitor by name for the express purpose of showing why the competitor is inferior to the product naming it.

This should not be confused with parody advertisements, where a fictional product is being advertised for the purpose of poking fun at the particular advertisement, nor should it be confused with the use of a coined brand name for the purpose of comparing the product without actually naming an actual competitor. ('Wikipedia tastes better and is less filling than the Encyclopedia Galactica.')

In the 1980s, during what has been referred to as the cola wars, soft-drink manufacturer Pepsi ran a series of advertisements where people, caught on hidden camera, in a blind taste test, chose Pepsi over rival Coca-Cola.

 a. Heavy-up
 b. Comparative advertising
 c. Cost per conversion
 d. GL-70

15. _____ is a broad label that refers to any individuals or households that use goods and services generated within the economy. The concept of a _____ is used in different contexts, so that the usage and significance of the term may vary.

A _____ is a person who uses any product or service.

 a. Power III
 b. Consumer
 c. 6-3-5 Brainwriting
 d. 180SearchAssistant

16. _____ is a business management strategy aimed at embedding awareness of quality in all organizational processes. _____ has been widely used in manufacturing, education, call centers, government, and service industries, as well as NASA space and science programs.

When used together as a phrase, the three words in this expression have the following meanings:

- Total: Involving the entire organization, supply chain, and/or product life cycle
- Quality: With its usual definitions, with all its complexities
- Management: The system of managing with steps like Plan, Organize, Control, Lead, Staff, provisioning and organizing.

As defined by the International Organization for Standardization (ISO):

> '_____ is a management approach for an organization, centered on quality, based on the participation of all its members and aiming at long-term success through customer satisfaction, and benefits to all members of the organization and to society.' ISO 8402:1994

One major aim is to reduce variation from every process so that greater consistency of effort is obtained. (Royse, D., Thyer, B., Padgett D., ' Logan T., 2006)

In Japan, _____ comprises four process steps, namely:

1. Kaizen - Focuses on 'Continuous Process Improvement', to make processes visible, repeatable and measurable.
2. Atarimae Hinshitsu - The idea that 'things will work as they are supposed to'.
3. Kansei - Examining the way the user applies the product leads to improvement in the product itself.
4. Miryokuteki Hinshitsu - The idea that 'things should have an aesthetic quality' (for example, a pen will write in a way that is pleasing to the writer.)

_____ requires that the company maintain this quality standard in all aspects of its business. This requires ensuring that things are done right the first time and that defects and waste are eliminated from operations.

a. 180SearchAssistant
b. 6-3-5 Brainwriting
c. Power III
d. Total quality management

52 *Chapter 9. Survey Research: Basic Methods of Communication with Respondents*

1. _____ is an advertisement in which a particular product specifically mentions a competitor by name for the express purpose of showing why the competitor is inferior to the product naming it.

This should not be confused with parody advertisements, where a fictional product is being advertised for the purpose of poking fun at the particular advertisement, nor should it be confused with the use of a coined brand name for the purpose of comparing the product without actually naming an actual competitor. ('Wikipedia tastes better and is less filling than the Encyclopedia Galactica.')

In the 1980s, during what has been referred to as the cola wars, soft-drink manufacturer Pepsi ran a series of advertisements where people, caught on hidden camera, in a blind taste test, chose Pepsi over rival Coca-Cola.

   a. Cost per conversion　　　　　　　　　b. Heavy-up
   c. Comparative advertising　　　　　　　d. GL-70

2. In probability theory and statistics, _____ indicates the strength and direction of a linear relationship between two random variables. That is in contrast with the usage of the term in colloquial speech, denoting any relationship, not necessarily linear. In general statistical usage, _____ or co-relation refers to the departure of two random variables from independence.
   a. Correlation　　　　　　　　　　　　　b. Probability
   c. Mean　　　　　　　　　　　　　　　　d. Frequency distribution

3. _____ describes the situation when output from (or information about the result of) an event or phenomenon in the past will influence the same event/phenomenon in the present or future. When an event is part of a chain of cause-and-effect that forms a circuit or loop, then the event is said to 'feed back' into itself.

_____ is also a synonym for:

- _____ Signal; the information about the initial event that is the basis for subsequent modification of the event.
- _____ Loop; the causal path that leads from the initial generation of the _____ signal to the subsequent modification of the event.

_____ is a mechanism, process or signal that is looped back to control a system within itself. Such a loop is called a _____ loop.

   a. 180SearchAssistant　　　　　　　　　b. Power III
   c. 6-3-5 Brainwriting　　　　　　　　　　d. Feedback

4. _____ is a sales technique in which a salesperson walks from one door of a house to another trying to sell a product or service to the general public. A variant of this involves cold calling first, when another sales representative attempts to gain agreement that a salesperson should visit. _____ selling is usually conducted in the afternoon hours, when the majority of people are at home.
   a. Marketing management　　　　　　　b. Fast moving consumer goods
   c. Door-to-door　　　　　　　　　　　　d. Performance-based advertising

Chapter 9. Survey Research: Basic Methods of Communication with Respondents

5. A personal and cultural _____ is a relative ethic _____, an assumption upon which implementation can be extrapolated. A _____ system is a set of consistent _____s and measures that is soo not true. A principle _____ is a foundation upon which other _____s and measures of integrity are based.
   a. Package-on-Package
   b. Supreme Court of the United States
   c. Perceptual maps
   d. Value

6. In economics and sociology, an _____ is any factor (financial or non-financial) that enables or motivates a particular course of action, or counts as a reason for preferring one choice to the alternatives. It is an expectation that encourages people to behave in a certain way. Since human beings are purposeful creatures, the study of _____ structures is central to the study of all economic activity (both in terms of individual decision-making and in terms of co-operation and competition within a larger institutional structure.)
   a. Incentive
   b. AMAX
   c. ACNielsen
   d. ADTECH

7. The United States _____ is the government agency that is responsible for the United States Census. It also gathers other national demographic and economic data.
   a. Census Bureau
   b. Power III
   c. 6-3-5 Brainwriting
   d. 180SearchAssistant

8. _____ is a telephone surveying technique in which the interviewer follows a script provided by a software application. The software is able to customize the flow of the questionnaire based on the answers provided, as well as information already known about the participant.

CATI may function in the following manner

- A computerized questionnaire is administered to respondents over the telephone.
- The interviewer sits in front of a computer screen
- Upon command, the computer dials the telephone number to be called.
- When contact is made, the interviewer reads the questions posed on the computer screen and records the respondent's answers directly into the computer.
- Interim and update reports can be compiled instantaneously, as the data are being collected.
- CATI software has built-in logic, which also enhances data accuracy.
- The program will personalize questions and control for logically incorrect answers, such as percentage answers that do not add up to 100 percent.
- The software has built-in branching logic, which will skip questions that are not applicable or will probe for more detail when warranted.

   a. 6-3-5 Brainwriting
   b. Power III
   c. Computer-assisted telephone interviewing
   d. 180SearchAssistant

9. _____ is one of the four elements of marketing mix. An organization or set of organizations (go-betweens) involved in the process of making a product or service available for use or consumption by a consumer or business user.

The other three parts of the marketing mix are product, pricing, and promotion.

Chapter 9. Survey Research: Basic Methods of Communication with Respondents

a. Distribution
b. Comparison-Shopping agent
c. Better Living Through Chemistry
d. Japan Advertising Photographers' Association

10. A _____ is a research instrument consisting of a series of questions and other prompts for the purpose of gathering information from respondents. Although they are often designed for statistical analysis of the responses, this is not always the case. The _____ was invented by Sir Francis Galton.
a. Mystery shoppers
b. Questionnaire
c. Market research
d. Mystery shopping

11. _____ in survey research refers to the ratio of number of people who answered the survey divided by the number of people in the sample. It is usually expressed in the form of a percentage.

Example: if 1,000 surveys were sent by mail, and 257 were successfully completed and returned, then the _____ would be 25.7 %.

a. Sentence completion tests
b. Reference value
c. Power III
d. Response rate

12. In the Mediterranean Basin and the Near East, a _____ is a small, separated garden pavilion open on some or all sides. _____s were common in Persia, India, Pakistan, and in the Ottoman Empire from the 13th century onward. Today, there are many _____s in and around the TopkapÄ± Palace in Istanbul, and they are still a relatively common sight in Greece.
a. Kiosk
b. 6-3-5 Brainwriting
c. Power III
d. 180SearchAssistant

13. _____ a research method involving the use of questionnaires and/or statistical surveys to gather data about people and their thoughts and behaviours.
a. Z-test
b. Control chart
c. T-test
d. Survey research

14. _____ is a branch of philosophy which seeks to address questions about morality, such as how a moral outcome can be achieved in a specific situation (applied _____), how moral values should be determined (normative _____), what moral values people actually abide by (descriptive _____), what the fundamental semantic, ontological, and epistemic nature of _____ or morality is (meta-_____), and how moral capacity or moral agency develops and what its nature is (moral psychology.)

Socrates was one of the first Greek philosophers to encourage both scholars and the common citizen to turn their attention from the outside world to the condition of man. In this view, Knowledge having a bearing on human life was placed highest, all other knowledge being secondary.

a. ACNielsen
b. AMAX
c. Ethics
d. ADTECH

1. _____ is either an activity of a living being (such as a human), consisting of receiving knowledge of the outside world through the senses, or the recording of data using scientific instruments. The term may also refer to any datum collected during this activity.

The scientific method requires _____s of nature to formulate and test hypotheses.

a. ADTECH
b. AMAX
c. Observation
d. ACNielsen

2. _____ is a measure of the strength of a brand, product, service relative to competitive offerings. There is often a geographic element to the competitive landscape. In defining _____, you must see to what extent a product, brand, or firm controls a product category in a given geographic area.

a. Productivity
b. Discretionary spending
c. Market dominance
d. Market system

3. _____ is a broad label that refers to any individuals or households that use goods and services generated within the economy. The concept of a _____ is used in different contexts, so that the usage and significance of the term may vary.

A _____ is a person who uses any product or service.

a. 180SearchAssistant
b. Power III
c. 6-3-5 Brainwriting
d. Consumer

4. _____ is a standard point of view or personal prejudice. especially when the tendency interferes with the ability to be impartial, unprejudiced, or objective. The term _____ed is used to describe an action, judgment, or other outcome influenced by a prejudged perspective.

a. Power III
b. Bias
c. 6-3-5 Brainwriting
d. 180SearchAssistant

5. In probability theory and statistics, _____ indicates the strength and direction of a linear relationship between two random variables. That is in contrast with the usage of the term in colloquial speech, denoting any relationship, not necessarily linear. In general statistical usage, _____ or co-relation refers to the departure of two random variables from independence.

a. Frequency distribution
b. Probability
c. Mean
d. Correlation

6. _____ is a methodology in the social sciences for studying the content of communication. Earl Babbie defines it as 'the study of recorded human communications, such as books, websites, paintings and laws.' It is most commonly used by researchers in the social sciences to analyze recorded transcripts of interviews with participants.

_____ is also considered a scholarly methodology in the humanities by which texts are studied as to authorship, authenticity, of meaning.

a. 6-3-5 Brainwriting
b. 180SearchAssistant
c. Power III
d. Content analysis

Chapter 10. Observation

7. _____ is a way of measuring the success of an online advertising campaign. A CTR is obtained by dividing the number of users who clicked on an ad on a web page by the number of times the ad was delivered (impressions.) For example, if a banner ad was delivered 100 times (impressions delivered) and one person clicked on it (clicks recorded), then the resulting CTR would be 1 percent.

   a. JICIMS
   b. Web analytics
   c. Display advertising
   d. Click-through rate

8. Human beings are also considered to be _____ because they have the ability to change raw materials into valuable _____. The term Human _____ can also be defined as the skills, energies, talents, abilities and knowledge that are used for the production of goods or the rendering of services. While taking into account human beings as _____, the following things have to be kept in mind:

   - The size of the population
   - The capabilities of the individuals in that population

   Many _____ cannot be consumed in their original form. They have to be processed in order to change them into more usable commodities.

   a. Resources
   b. Power III
   c. 6-3-5 Brainwriting
   d. 180SearchAssistant

9. In statistics, analysis of variance (_____) is a collection of statistical models, and their associated procedures, in which the observed variance is partitioned into components due to different explanatory variables. In its simplest form _____ gives a statistical test of whether the means of several groups are all equal, and therefore generalizes Student's two-sample t-test to more than two groups.

   There are three conceptual classes of such models:

   1. Fixed-effects models assumes that the data came from normal populations which may differ only in their means. (Model 1)
   2. Random effects models assume that the data describe a hierarchy of different populations whose differences are constrained by the hierarchy. (Model 2)
   3. Mixed-effect models describe situations where both fixed and random effects are present. (Model 3)

   In practice, there are several types of _____ depending on the number of treatments and the way they are applied to the subjects in the experiment:

   - One-way _____ is used to test for differences among two or more independent groups. Typically, however, the one-way _____ is used to test for differences among at least three groups, since the two-group case can be covered by a T-test (Gossett, 1908.)

   a. ADTECH
   b. AMAX
   c. ANOVA
   d. ACNielsen

10. _____ is that part of statistical practice concerned with the selection of individual observations intended to yield some knowledge about a population of concern, especially for the purposes of statistical inference. Each observation measures one or more properties (weight, location, etc.) of an observable entity enumerated to distinguish objects or individuals.
   a. AStore
   b. Sports Marketing Group
   c. Richard Buckminster 'Bucky' Fuller
   d. Sampling

11. A _____ is any statistical test for which the distribution of the test statistic under the null hypothesis can be approximated by a normal distribution. Since many test statistics are approximately normally distributed for large samples (due to the central limit theorem), many statistical tests can be performed as approximate _____ s if the sample size is not too small. In addition, some statistical tests such as comparisons of means between two samples, or a comparison of the mean of one sample to a given constant, are exact _____ s under certain assumptions.
   a. Null hypothesis
   b. Z-test
   c. Confounding variables
   d. Sample size

Chapter 11. Experimental Research: An Overview

1. _____ is that part of statistical practice concerned with the selection of individual observations intended to yield some knowledge about a population of concern, especially for the purposes of statistical inference. Each observation measures one or more properties (weight, location, etc.) of an observable entity enumerated to distinguish objects or individuals.
   a. AStore
   b. Sports Marketing Group
   c. Richard Buckminster 'Bucky' Fuller
   d. Sampling

2. A personal and cultural _____ is a relative ethic _____, an assumption upon which implementation can be extrapolated. A _____ system is a set of consistent _____s and measures that is soo not true. A principle _____ is a foundation upon which other _____s and measures of integrity are based.
   a. Perceptual maps
   b. Supreme Court of the United States
   c. Package-on-Package
   d. Value

3. A number of different _____s are indicated below.

   - Randomized controlled trial
     - Double-blind randomized trial
     - Single-blind randomized trial
     - Non-blind trial
   - Nonrandomized trial (quasi-experiment)
     - Interrupted time series design (measures on a sample or a series of samples from the same population are obtained several times before and after a manipulated event or a naturally occurring event) - considered a type of quasi-experiment
   - Cohort study
     - Prospective cohort
     - Retrospective cohort
     - Time series study
   - Case-control study
     - Nested case-control study
   - Cross-sectional study
     - Community survey (a type of cross-sectional study)

   When choosing a _____, many factors must be taken into account. Different types of studies are subject to different types of bias. For example, recall bias is likely to occur in cross-sectional or case-control studies where subjects are asked to recall exposure to risk factors.

   a. Longitudinal studies
   b. Study design
   c. 180SearchAssistant
   d. Power III

4. _____s are used in open sentences. For instance, in the formula $x + 1 = 5$, x is a _____ which represents an 'unknown' number. _____s are often represented by letters of the Roman alphabet, or those of other alphabets, such as Greek, and use other special symbols.
   a. Personalization
   b. Variable
   c. Quantitative
   d. Book of business

Chapter 11. Experimental Research: An Overview

5. Human beings are also considered to be _____ because they have the ability to change raw materials into valuable _____. The term Human _____ can also be defined as the skills, energies, talents, abilities and knowledge that are used for the production of goods or the rendering of services. While taking into account human beings as _____, the following things have to be kept in mind:

- The size of the population
- The capabilities of the individuals in that population

Many _____ cannot be consumed in their original form. They have to be processed in order to change them into more usable commodities.

a. 180SearchAssistant
c. 6-3-5 Brainwriting
b. Power III
d. Resources

6. In statistics, an _____ is a term in a statistical model added when the effect of two or more variables is not simply additive. Such a term reflects that the effect of one variable depends on the values of one or more other variables.

Thus, for a response Y and two variables x_1 and x_2 an additive model would be:

$$Y = ax_1 + bx_2 + \text{error}$$

In contrast to this,

$$Y = ax_1 + bx_2 + c(x_1 \times x_2) + \text{error},$$

is an example of a model with an _____ between variables x_1 and x_2 ('error' refers to the random variable whose value by which y differs from the expected value of y.)

a. ACNielsen
c. ADTECH
b. AMAX
d. Interaction

7. _____ is an advertisement in which a particular product specifically mentions a competitor by name for the express purpose of showing why the competitor is inferior to the product naming it.

This should not be confused with parody advertisements, where a fictional product is being advertised for the purpose of poking fun at the particular advertisement, nor should it be confused with the use of a coined brand name for the purpose of comparing the product without actually naming an actual competitor. ('Wikipedia tastes better and is less filling than the Encyclopedia Galactica.')

In the 1980s, during what has been referred to as the cola wars, soft-drink manufacturer Pepsi ran a series of advertisements where people, caught on hidden camera, in a blind taste test, chose Pepsi over rival Coca-Cola.

a. Heavy-up
b. Cost per conversion
c. Comparative advertising
d. GL-70

8. A _____ is a relatively new executive level position at a corporation, company, organization typically reporting directly to the CEO or board of directors. The _____ is responsible for a brand's image, experience, and promise, and propagating it throughout all aspects of the company. The brand officer oversees marketing, advertising, design, public relations and customer service departments.
   a. Chief executive officer
   b. Power III
   c. Financial analyst
   d. Chief brand officer

9. _____ is a broad label that refers to any individuals or households that use goods and services generated within the economy. The concept of a _____ is used in different contexts, so that the usage and significance of the term may vary.

A _____ is a person who uses any product or service.

   a. 180SearchAssistant
   b. 6-3-5 Brainwriting
   c. Power III
   d. Consumer

10. The terms '_____' and 'independent variable' are used in similar but subtly different ways in mathematics and statistics as part of the standard terminology in those subjects. They are used to distinguish between two types of quantities being considered, separating them into those available at the start of a process and those being created by it, where the latter (_____s) are dependent on the former (independent variables.)

In traditional calculus, a function is defined as a relation between two terms called variables because their values vary.

   a. Field experiment
   b. Power III
   c. 180SearchAssistant
   d. Dependent variable

11. _____s are biases in measurement which lead to the situation where the mean of many separate measurements differs significantly from the actual value of the measured attribute. All measurements are prone to _____s, often of several different types. Sources of _____ may be imperfect calibration of measurement instruments, changes in the environment which interfere with the measurement process and sometimes imperfect methods of observation can be either zero error or percentage error.
   a. Power III
   b. 180SearchAssistant
   c. Systematic bias
   d. Systematic error

12. In the mathematical discipline of graph theory a _____ or edge-independent set in a graph is a set of edges without common vertices. It may also be an entire graph consisting of edges without common vertices.

Given a graph G = (V,E), a _____ M in G is a set of pairwise non-adjacent edges; that is, no two edges share a common vertex.

Chapter 11. Experimental Research: An Overview

a. Power III
c. 180SearchAssistant
b. 6-3-5 Brainwriting
d. Matching

13. _____ is the process of making something random; this means:

- Generating a random permutation of a sequence (such as when shuffling cards.)
- Selecting a random sample of a population (important in statistical sampling.)
- Generating random numbers: see Random number generation.
- Transforming a data stream using a scrambler in telecommunications.

_____ is used extensively in the field of gambling (or generally being random.) Imperfect _____ may allow a skilled gambler to have an advantage, so much research has been devoted to effective _____. A classic example of _____ is shuffling playing cards.

_____ is a core principle in the statistical theory of design of experiments.

a. Standard deviation
c. Randomization
b. Statistics
d. Sample size

14. _____ is a telephone surveying technique in which the interviewer follows a script provided by a software application. The software is able to customize the flow of the questionnaire based on the answers provided, as well as information already known about the participant.

CATI may function in the following manner

- A computerized questionnaire is administered to respondents over the telephone.
- The interviewer sits in front of a computer screen
- Upon command, the computer dials the telephone number to be called.
- When contact is made, the interviewer reads the questions posed on the computer screen and records the respondent's answers directly into the computer.
- Interim and update reports can be compiled instantaneously, as the data are being collected.
- CATI software has built-in logic, which also enhances data accuracy.
- The program will personalize questions and control for logically incorrect answers, such as percentage answers that do not add up to 100 percent.
- The software has built-in branching logic, which will skip questions that are not applicable or will probe for more detail when warranted.

a. Power III
c. 6-3-5 Brainwriting
b. Computer-assisted telephone interviewing
d. 180SearchAssistant

15. _____ are variables other than the independent variable that may bear any effect on the behavior of the subject being studied.

_____ are often classified into three main types:

1. Subject variables, which are the characteristics of the individuals being studied that might affect their actions. These variables include age, gender, health status, mood, background, etc.
2. Experimental variables are characteristics of the persons conducting the experiment which might influence how a person behaves. Gender, the presence of racial discrimination, language, or other factors may qualify as such variables.
3. Situational variables are features of the environment in which the study or research was conducted, which have a bearing on the outcome of the experiment in a negative way. Included are the air temperature, level of activity, lighting, and the time of day.

There are two strategies of controlling _____. Either a potentially influential variable is kept the same for all subjects in the research, or they balance the variables in a group.

Take for example an experiment, in which a salesperson sells clothing on a door-to-door basis.

a. AMAX
c. ACNielsen
b. Extraneous variables
d. ADTECH

16. _____ is a standard point of view or personal prejudice. especially when the tendency interferes with the ability to be impartial, unprejudiced, or objective. The term _____ed is used to describe an action, judgment, or other outcome influenced by a prejudged perspective.
   a. 180SearchAssistant
   c. Power III
   b. 6-3-5 Brainwriting
   d. Bias

17. In economics, _____ is the desire to own something and the ability to pay for it. The term _____ signifies the ability or the willingness to buy a particular commodity at a given point of time .

   a. Market dominance
   c. Discretionary spending
   b. Market system
   d. Demand

18. In research, and particularly psychology, _____ refers to an experimental artifact where participants form an interpretation of the experiment's purpose and unconsciously change their behavior accordingly. Pioneering research was conducted on _____ by Martin Orne. Typically, they are considered a confounding variable, exerting an effect on behavior other than that intended by the experimenter.
   a. 180SearchAssistant
   c. 6-3-5 Brainwriting
   b. Demand characteristics
   d. Power III

19. The _____ is a form of reactivity, The term was coined in 1955 by Henry A. Landsberger when analyzing older experiments from 1924-1932 at the Hawthorne Works (outside Chicago.) Landsberger defined the _____ as:

   • a short-term improvement caused by observing worker performance.

Earlier researchers had concluded the short-term improvement was caused by teamwork when workers saw themselves as part of a study group or team. Others have broadened the definition to mean that people's behavior and performance change following any new or increased attention. Hence, the term _____ no longer has a specific definition.

a. 180SearchAssistant
b. Power III
c. 6-3-5 Brainwriting
d. Hawthorne effect

20. In probability theory and statistics, _____ indicates the strength and direction of a linear relationship between two random variables. That is in contrast with the usage of the term in colloquial speech, denoting any relationship, not necessarily linear. In general statistical usage, _____ or co-relation refers to the departure of two random variables from independence.
a. Frequency distribution
b. Probability
c. Mean
d. Correlation

21. _____ is a branch of philosophy which seeks to address questions about morality, such as how a moral outcome can be achieved in a specific situation (applied _____), how moral values should be determined (normative _____), what moral values people actually abide by (descriptive _____), what the fundamental semantic, ontological, and epistemic nature of _____ or morality is (meta-_____), and how moral capacity or moral agency develops and what its nature is (moral psychology.)

Socrates was one of the first Greek philosophers to encourage both scholars and the common citizen to turn their attention from the outside world to the condition of man. In this view, Knowledge having a bearing on human life was placed highest, all other knowledge being secondary.

a. ACNielsen
b. AMAX
c. ADTECH
d. Ethics

22. _____ is a mathematical science pertaining to the collection, analysis, interpretation or explanation, and presentation of data. It also provides tools for prediction and forecasting based on data. It is applicable to a wide variety of academic disciplines, from the natural and social sciences to the humanities, government and business.
a. Statistics
b. Type I error
c. Median
d. Null hypothesis

23. A _____ applies the scientific method to experimentally examine an intervention in the real world (or as many experimental economists like to say, naturally-occurring environments) rather than in the laboratory. _____s, like lab experiments, generally randomize subjects (or other sampling units) into treatment and control groups and compare outcomes between these groups. Clinical trials of pharmaceuticals are one example of _____s.
a. Power III
b. 180SearchAssistant
c. Response variable
d. Field experiment

24. _____ is the validity of (causal) inferences in scientific studies, usually based on experiments as experimental validity .

Chapter 11. Experimental Research: An Overview

Inferences are said to possess _____ if a causal relation between two variables is properly demonstrated. A causal inference may be based on a relation when three criteria are satisfied:

1. the 'cause' precedes the 'effect' in time (temporal precedence),
2. the 'cause' and the 'effect' are related (covariation), and
3. there are no plausible alternative explanations for the observed covariation (nonspuriousness).

In scientific experimental settings, researchers often manipulate a variable (the independent variable) to see what effect it has on a second variable (the dependent variable) For example, a researcher might, for different experimental groups, manipulate the dosage of a particular drug between groups to see what effect it has on health. In this example, the researcher wants to make a causal inference, namely, that different doses of the drug may be held responsible for observed changes or differences.

a. ADTECH
c. ACNielsen
b. AMAX
d. Internal validity

25. In economics, an externality or spillover of an economic transaction is an impact on a party that is not directly involved in the transaction. In such a case, prices do not reflect the full costs or benefits in production or consumption of a product or service. A positive impact is called an _____ benefit, while a negative impact is called an _____ cost.

a. External
c. AMAX
b. ACNielsen
d. ADTECH

26. _____ is the validity of generalized (causal) inferences in scientific studies, usually based on experiments as experimental validity.

Inferences about cause-effect relationships based on a specific scientific study are said to possess _____ if they may be generalized from the unique and idiosyncratic settings, procedures and participants to other populations and conditions Causal inferences said to possess high degrees of _____ can reasonably be expected to apply (a) to the target population of the study (i.e. from which the sample was drawn) (also referred to as population validity), and (b) to the universe of other populations (e.g. across time and space.)

The most common loss of _____ comes from the fact that experiments using human participants often employ small samples obtained from a single geographic location or with idiosyncratic features (e.g. volunteers.)

a. AMAX
c. ACNielsen
b. External validity
d. ADTECH

Chapter 12. Test-Markets and Experimental Design

1. _____ is the process of estimation in unknown situations. Prediction is a similar, but more general term. Both can refer to estimation of time series, cross-sectional or longitudinal data.
   a. 180SearchAssistant
   b. Power III
   c. 6-3-5 Brainwriting
   d. Forecasting

2. _____ is defined by the American _____ Association as the activity, set of institutions, and processes for creating, communicating, delivering, and exchanging offerings that have value for customers, clients, partners, and society at large. The term developed from the original meaning which referred literally to going to market, as in shopping, or going to a market to sell goods or services.

   _____ practice tends to be seen as a creative industry, which includes advertising, distribution and selling.

   a. Customer acquisition management
   b. Marketing
   c. Product naming
   d. Marketing myopia

3. _____ is a business discipline which is focused on the practical application of marketing techniques and the management of a firm's marketing resources and activities. Marketing managers are often responsible for influencing the level, timing, and composition of customer demand accepted definition of the term. In part, this is because the role of a marketing manager can vary significantly based on a business' size, corporate culture, and industry context.
   a. Business structure
   b. Performance-based advertising
   c. Marketing Management
   d. Door-to-door

4. The _____ is generally accepted as the use and specification of the four p's describing the strategic position of a product in the marketplace. One version of the origins of the _____ starts in 1948 when James Culliton said that a marketing decision should be a result of something similar to a recipe. This version continued in 1953 when Neil Borden, in his American Marketing Association presidential address, took the recipe idea one step further and coined the term 'Marketing-Mix'.
   a. Marketing mix
   b. Power III
   c. 6-3-5 Brainwriting
   d. 180SearchAssistant

5. A _____, in the field of business and marketing, is a geographic region or demographic group used to gauge the viability of a product or service in the mass market prior to a wide scale roll-out. The criteria used to judge the acceptability of a _____ region or group include:

   1. a population that is demographically similar to the proposed target market; and
   2. relative isolation from densely populated media markets so that advertising to the test audience can be efficient and economical.

Chapter 12. Test-Markets and Experimental Design

The _____ ideally aims to duplicate 'everything' - promotion and distribution as well as `product' - on a smaller scale. The technique replicates, typically in one area, what is planned to occur in a national launch; and the results are very carefully monitored, so that they can be extrapolated to projected national results. The `area' may be any one of the following:

- Television area
- Test town
- Residential neighborhood
- Test site

A number of decisions have to be taken about any _____:

- Which _____?
- What is to be tested?
- How long a test?
- What are the success criteria?

The simple go or no-go decision, together with the related reduction of risk, is normally the main justification for the expense of _____s. At the same time, however, such _____s can be used to test specific elements of a new product's marketing mix; possibly the version of the product itself, the promotional message and media spend, the distribution channels and the price.

a. Power III
c. 180SearchAssistant
b. Preadolescence
d. Test market

6. Procter is a surname, and may also refer to:

- Bryan Waller Procter (pseud. Barry Cornwall), English poet
- Goodwin Procter, American law firm
- _____, consumer products multinational

a. Flyer
c. Convergent
b. Procter ' Gamble
d. Black PRies

7. In business and engineering, new _____ is the term used to describe the complete process of bringing a new product or service to market. There are two parallel paths involved in the Nproduct development process: one involves the idea generation, product design, and detail engineering; the other involves market research and marketing analysis. Companies typically see new _____ as the first stage in generating and commercializing new products within the overall strategic process of product life cycle management used to maintain or grow their market share.

a. New product development
c. Product development
b. Specification tree
d. New product screening

8. A _____ applies the scientific method to experimentally examine an intervention in the real world (or as many experimental economists like to say, naturally-occurring environments) rather than in the laboratory. _____s, like lab experiments, generally randomize subjects (or other sampling units) into treatment and control groups and compare outcomes between these groups. Clinical trials of pharmaceuticals are one example of _____s.
   a. 180SearchAssistant
   b. Response variable
   c. Power III
   d. Field experiment

9. Human beings are also considered to be _____ because they have the ability to change raw materials into valuable _____. The term Human _____ can also be defined as the skills, energies, talents, abilities and knowledge that are used for the production of goods or the rendering of services. While taking into account human beings as _____, the following things have to be kept in mind:

   - The size of the population
   - The capabilities of the individuals in that population

   Many _____ cannot be consumed in their original form. They have to be processed in order to change them into more usable commodities.

   a. 6-3-5 Brainwriting
   b. 180SearchAssistant
   c. Power III
   d. Resources

10. _____ is one of the four growth strategies of the Product-Market Growth Matrix defined by Ansoff. _____ occurs when a company enters/penetrates a market with current products. The best way to achieve this is by gaining competitors' customers (part of their market share.)
    a. Pasar pagi
    b. Market penetration
    c. Marketization
    d. Horizontal market

11. _____, in strategic management and marketing, is the percentage or proportion of the total available market or market segment that is being serviced by a company. It can be expressed as a company's sales revenue (from that market) divided by the total sales revenue available in that market. It can also be expressed as a company's unit sales volume (in a market) divided by the total volume of units sold in that market.
    a. Customer relationship management
    b. Cyberdoc
    c. Market share
    d. Demand generation

12. _____ is a broad label that refers to any individuals or households that use goods and services generated within the economy. The concept of a _____ is used in different contexts, so that the usage and significance of the term may vary.

    A _____ is a person who uses any product or service.

    a. Power III
    b. Consumer
    c. 6-3-5 Brainwriting
    d. 180SearchAssistant

13. _____ refer to a collection of facts usually collected as the result of experience, observation or experiment or a set of premises. This may consist of numbers, words particularly as measurements or observations of a set of variables. _____ are often viewed as a lowest level of abstraction from which information and knowledge are derived.

a. Pearson product-moment correlation coefficient
b. Sample size
c. Data
d. Mean

14. _____ is the imitation of some real thing, state of affairs, or process. The act of simulating something generally entails representing certain key characteristics or behaviors of a selected physical or abstract system.

_____ is used in many contexts, including the modeling of natural systems or human systems in order to gain insight into their functioning.

a. Simulation
b. 180SearchAssistant
c. Power III
d. 6-3-5 Brainwriting

15. _____ is that part of statistical practice concerned with the selection of individual observations intended to yield some knowledge about a population of concern, especially for the purposes of statistical inference. Each observation measures one or more properties (weight, location, etc.) of an observable entity enumerated to distinguish objects or individuals.

a. Richard Buckminster 'Bucky' Fuller
b. Sampling
c. Sports Marketing Group
d. AStore

16. In the design of experiments, _____ are for studying the effects of one primary factor without the need to take other nuisance factors into account The experiment compares the values of a response variable based on the different levels of that primary factor.

a. Comprehensive,
b. Completely randomized designs
c. Geo
d. Just-In-Case

17. _____,, is a common tool in the retail industry to create the look of a perfectly stocked store by pulling all of the products on a display or shelf to the front, as well as downstacking all the canned and stacked items. It is also done to keep the store appearing neat and organized.

The workers who face commonly have jobs doing other things in the store such as customer service, stocking shelves, daytime cleaning, bagging and carryouts, etc.

a. Customer Experience Analytics
b. Foviance
c. Customer Integrated System
d. Facing

18. _____s are used in open sentences. For instance, in the formula x + 1 = 5, x is a _____ which represents an 'unknown' number. _____s are often represented by letters of the Roman alphabet, or those of other alphabets, such as Greek, and use other special symbols.

a. Personalization
b. Quantitative
c. Book of business
d. Variable

19. In statistics, an _____ is a term in a statistical model added when the effect of two or more variables is not simply additive. Such a term reflects that the effect of one variable depends on the values of one or more other variables.

Thus, for a response Y and two variables x_1 and x_2 an additive model would be:

$$Y = ax_1 + bx_2 + \text{error}$$

In contrast to this,

$$Y = ax_1 + bx_2 + c(x_1 \times x_2) + \text{error},$$

is an example of a model with an _____ between variables x_1 and x_2 ('error' refers to the random variable whose value by which y differs from the expected value of y.)

a. AMAX
c. ACNielsen
b. ADTECH
d. Interaction

1. The _____ is a global navigation satellite system (GNSS) developed by the United States Department of Defense and managed by the United States Air Force 50th Space Wing. It is the only fully functional GNSS in the world, can be used freely, and is often used by civilians for navigation purposes. It uses a constellation of between 24 and 32 Medium Earth Orbit satellites that transmit precise microwave signals, which allow _____ receivers to determine their current location, the time, and their velocity.
   a. Global positioning system
   b. 6-3-5 Brainwriting
   c. Power III
   d. 180SearchAssistant

2. _____ is a telephone surveying technique in which the interviewer follows a script provided by a software application. The software is able to customize the flow of the questionnaire based on the answers provided, as well as information already known about the participant.

   CATI may function in the following manner

   - A computerized questionnaire is administered to respondents over the telephone.
   - The interviewer sits in front of a computer screen
   - Upon command, the computer dials the telephone number to be called.
   - When contact is made, the interviewer reads the questions posed on the computer screen and records the respondent's answers directly into the computer.
   - Interim and update reports can be compiled instantaneously, as the data are being collected.
   - CATI software has built-in logic, which also enhances data accuracy.
   - The program will personalize questions and control for logically incorrect answers, such as percentage answers that do not add up to 100 percent.
   - The software has built-in branching logic, which will skip questions that are not applicable or will probe for more detail when warranted.

   a. 180SearchAssistant
   b. 6-3-5 Brainwriting
   c. Power III
   d. Computer-assisted telephone interviewing

3. _____ is defined by the American _____ Association as the activity, set of institutions, and processes for creating, communicating, delivering, and exchanging offerings that have value for customers, clients, partners, and society at large. The term developed from the original meaning which referred literally to going to market, as in shopping, or going to a market to sell goods or services.

   _____ practice tends to be seen as a creative industry, which includes advertising, distribution and selling.

   a. Marketing myopia
   b. Product naming
   c. Customer acquisition management
   d. Marketing

4. _____ is a business discipline which is focused on the practical application of marketing techniques and the management of a firm's marketing resources and activities. Marketing managers are often responsible for influencing the level, timing, and composition of customer demand accepted definition of the term. In part, this is because the role of a marketing manager can vary significantly based on a business' size, corporate culture, and industry context.
   a. Door-to-door
   b. Business structure
   c. Performance-based advertising
   d. Marketing Management

Chapter 13. Measurement

5. The '_____' is an expression which typically refers to the theory of scale types developed by the Harvard psychologist Stanley Smith Stevens In this article Stevens claimed that all measurement in science was conducted using four different types of numerical scales which he called 'nominal', 'ordinal', 'interval' and 'ratio'.
   a. Power III
   b. 180SearchAssistant
   c. 6-3-5 Brainwriting
   d. Levels of measurement

6. The _____ is a publication of the United States Census Bureau, an agency of the United States Department of Commerce. Published annually since 1878, the statistics describe social and economic conditions in the United States.

   In 1975 a two volume Historical Statistics of the United States, Colonial Times to 1970 Bicentennial Edition was published.

   a. 6-3-5 Brainwriting
   b. Power III
   c. 180SearchAssistant
   d. Statistical Abstract of the United States

7. _____ is a measure of the strength of a brand, product, service relative to competitive offerings. There is often a geographic element to the competitive landscape. In defining _____, you must see to what extent a product, brand, or firm controls a product category in a given geographic area.
   a. Market system
   b. Productivity
   c. Discretionary spending
   d. Market dominance

8. _____ is a broad label that refers to any individuals or households that use goods and services generated within the economy. The concept of a _____ is used in different contexts, so that the usage and significance of the term may vary.

   A _____ is a person who uses any product or service.

   a. Power III
   b. 6-3-5 Brainwriting
   c. Consumer
   d. 180SearchAssistant

9. A _____ is a psychometric scale commonly used in questionnaires, and is the most widely used scale in survey research. When responding to a Likert questionnaire item, respondents specify their level of agreement to a statement. The scale is named after its inventor, psychologist Rensis Likert.
   a. Semantic differential
   b. Factor analysis
   c. Likert scale
   d. Power III

10. Human beings are also considered to be _____ because they have the ability to change raw materials into valuable _____. The term Human _____ can also be defined as the skills, energies, talents, abilities and knowledge that are used for the production of goods or the rendering of services. While taking into account human beings as _____, the following things have to be kept in mind:

    - The size of the population
    - The capabilities of the individuals in that population

    Many _____ cannot be consumed in their original form. They have to be processed in order to change them into more usable commodities.

a. 180SearchAssistant
b. Power III
c. Resources
d. 6-3-5 Brainwriting

11. In statistics and research, _____ is a measure based on the correlations between different items on the same test (or the same subscale on a larger test.) It measures whether several items that propose to measure the same general construct produce similar scores. For example, if a respondent expressed agreement with the statements 'I like to ride bicycles' and 'I've enjoyed riding bicycles in the past', and disagreement with the statement 'I hate bicycles', this would be indicative of good _____ of the test.

a. ADTECH
b. AMAX
c. Internal consistency
d. ACNielsen

12. _____ is a statistical method used to examine how reliable a test is: A test is performed twice, e.g., the same test is given to a group of subjects at two different times. Each subject should score different than the other subjects, but if the test is reliable then each subject should score the same in both test.

Valentin Rousson, Theo Gasser, and Burkhardt Seifert, (2002) 'Assessing intrarater, interrater and _____ reliability of continuous measurements,' Statistics in Medicine 21:3431-3446.

a. 180SearchAssistant
b. 6-3-5 Brainwriting
c. Power III
d. Test-retest

13. In social science and psychometrics, _____ refers to whether a scale measures or correlates with a theorized psychological construct (such as 'fluid intelligence'.) It is related to the theoretical ideas behind the personality trait under consideration; a non-existent concept in the physical sense may be suggested as a method of organising how personality can be viewed. The unobservable idea of a unidimensional easier-to-harder dimension must be 'constructed' in the words of human language and graphics.

a. Construct validity
b. Discriminant validity
c. Predictive validity
d. Criterion validity

14. In psychometrics, _____ refers to the extent to which a measure represents all facets of a given social construct. For example, a depression scale may lack _____ if it only assesses the affective dimension of depression but fails to take into account the behavioral dimension. An element of subjectivity exists in relation to determining _____, which requires a degree of agreement about what a particular personality trait such as extraversion represents.

a. Convergent validity
b. Criterion validity
c. Predictive validity
d. Content validity

15. In the absence of a more specific context, convergence denotes the approach toward a definite value, as time goes on; or to a definite point, a common view or opinion, or toward a fixed or equilibrium state. _____ is the adjectival form, and also a noun meaning an iterative approximation.

In mathematics, convergence describes limiting behaviour, particularly of an infinite sequence or series, toward some limit.

a. Strict liability
b. Good things come to those who wait
c. Convergent
d. Geo

Chapter 13. Measurement

16. _____ is the degree to which an operation is similar to (converges on) other operations that it theoretically should also be similar to. For instance, to show the _____ of a test of mathematics skills, the scores on the test can be correlated with scores on other tests that are also designed to measure basic mathematics ability. High correlations between the test scores would be evidence of a _____.
    a. Convergent validity
    b. Content validity
    c. Discriminant validity
    d. Criterion validity

17. In psychometrics, _____ is a measure of how well one variable or set of variables predicts an outcome based on information from other variables, and will be achieved if a set of measures from a personality test relate to a behavioral criterion that psychologists agree on. A typical way to achieve this is in relation to the extent to which a score on a personality test can predict future performance or behaviour. Another way involves correlating test scores with another established test that also measures the same personality characteristic.
    a. Convergent validity
    b. Predictive validity
    c. Criterion validity
    d. Construct validity

18. In algebra, the _____ of a polynomial with real or complex coefficients is a certain expression in the coefficients of the polynomial which is equal to zero if and only if the polynomial has a multiple root (i.e. a root with multiplicity greater than one) in the complex numbers. For example, the _____ of the quadratic polynomial

$$ax^2 + bx + c \text{ is } b^2 - 4ac.$$

The _____ of the cubic polynomial

$$ax^3 + bx^2 + cx + d \text{ is } b^2c^2 - 4ac^3 - 4b^3d - 27a^2d^2 + 18abcd.$$

   a. Consumption Map
   b. Flighting
   c. Lifestyle center
   d. Discriminant

19. _____ describes the degree to which the operationalization is not similar to (diverges from) other operationalizations that it theoretically should not be similar to.

Campbell and Fiske (1959) introduced the concept of _____ within their discussion on evaluating test validity. They stressed the importance of using both discriminant and convergent validation techniques when assessing new tests.

   a. Predictive validity
   b. Criterion validity
   c. Convergent validity
   d. Discriminant validity

20. _____ is a property of a test intended to measure something. The test is said to have _____ if it 'looks like' it is going to measure what it is supposed to measure. For instance, if you prepare a test to measure whether students can perform multiplication, and the people you show it to all agree that it looks like a good test of multiplication ability, you have shown the _____ of your test.
   a. Selective distortion
   b. Face validity
   c. 180SearchAssistant
   d. Power III

21. _____ a research method involving the use of questionnaires and/or statistical surveys to gather data about people and their thoughts and behaviours.
   a. T-test
   b. Survey research
   c. Control chart
   d. Z-test

Chapter 14. Attitude Measurement

1. A _____ is a psychometric scale commonly used in questionnaires, and is the most widely used scale in survey research. When responding to a Likert questionnaire item, respondents specify their level of agreement to a statement. The scale is named after its inventor, psychologist Rensis Likert.
   a. Factor analysis
   b. Power III
   c. Likert scale
   d. Semantic differential

2. _____ is the ability of an individual or group to seclude themselves or information about themselves and thereby reveal themselves selectively. The boundaries and content of what is considered private differ among cultures and individuals, but share basic common themes. _____ is sometimes related to anonymity, the wish to remain unnoticed or unidentified in the public realm.
   a. Power III
   b. 6-3-5 Brainwriting
   c. 180SearchAssistant
   d. Privacy

3. A personal and cultural _____ is a relative ethic _____, an assumption upon which implementation can be extrapolated. A _____ system is a set of consistent _____s and measures that is soo not true. A principle _____ is a foundation upon which other _____s and measures of integrity are based.
   a. Perceptual maps
   b. Value
   c. Supreme Court of the United States
   d. Package-on-Package

4. _____ is a type of a rating scale designed to measure the connotative meaning of objects, events, and concepts. The connotations are used to derive the attitude towards the given object, event or concept.

   Osgood's _____ was designed to measure the connotative meaning of concepts.

   a. Factor analysis
   b. Semantic differential
   c. Power III
   d. Likert scale

5. _____ is a telephone surveying technique in which the interviewer follows a script provided by a software application. The software is able to customize the flow of the questionnaire based on the answers provided, as well as information already known about the participant.

CATI may function in the following manner

- A computerized questionnaire is administered to respondents over the telephone.
- The interviewer sits in front of a computer screen
- Upon command, the computer dials the telephone number to be called.
- When contact is made, the interviewer reads the questions posed on the computer screen and records the respondent's answers directly into the computer.
- Interim and update reports can be compiled instantaneously, as the data are being collected.
- CATI software has built-in logic, which also enhances data accuracy.
- The program will personalize questions and control for logically incorrect answers, such as percentage answers that do not add up to 100 percent.
- The software has built-in branching logic, which will skip questions that are not applicable or will probe for more detail when warranted.

a. 180SearchAssistant
b. 6-3-5 Brainwriting
c. Computer-assisted telephone interviewing
d. Power III

6. The _____ is a global navigation satellite system (GNSS) developed by the United States Department of Defense and managed by the United States Air Force 50th Space Wing. It is the only fully functional GNSS in the world, can be used freely, and is often used by civilians for navigation purposes. It uses a constellation of between 24 and 32 Medium Earth Orbit satellites that transmit precise microwave signals, which allow _____ receivers to determine their current location, the time, and their velocity.

a. Global positioning system
b. 180SearchAssistant
c. 6-3-5 Brainwriting
d. Power III

7. The _____ is a form of reactivity, The term was coined in 1955 by Henry A. Landsberger when analyzing older experiments from 1924-1932 at the Hawthorne Works (outside Chicago.) Landsberger defined the _____ as:

- a short-term improvement caused by observing worker performance.

Earlier researchers had concluded the short-term improvement was caused by teamwork when workers saw themselves as part of a study group or team. Others have broadened the definition to mean that people's behavior and performance change following any new or increased attention. Hence, the term _____ no longer has a specific definition.

a. 180SearchAssistant
b. Power III
c. 6-3-5 Brainwriting
d. Hawthorne effect

8. _____ is a mathematical science pertaining to the collection, analysis, interpretation or explanation, and presentation of data. It also provides tools for prediction and forecasting based on data. It is applicable to a wide variety of academic disciplines, from the natural and social sciences to the humanities, government and business.

a. Null hypothesis
b. Type I error
c. Median
d. Statistics

9. In environmental modeling and especially in hydrology, a _____ model means a model that is acceptably consistent with observed natural processes, i.e. that simulates well, for example, observed river discharge. It is a key concept of the so-called Generalized Likelihood Uncertainty Estimation (GLUE) methodology to quantify how uncertain environmental predictions are.

a. 6-3-5 Brainwriting
b. Behavioral
c. Power III
d. 180SearchAssistant

10. In grammar, the _____ is the form of an adjective or adverb which denotes the degree or grade by which a person, thing and is used in this context with a subordinating conjunction, such as than, as...as, etc.

The structure of a _____ in English consists normally of the positive form of the adjective or adverb, plus the suffix -er e.g. 'he is taller than his father is', or 'the village is less picturesque than the town nearby'.

a. 6-3-5 Brainwriting
b. Power III
c. 180SearchAssistant
d. Comparative

11. The U.S. _____ is an agency of the United States Department of Health and Human Services and is responsible for regulating and supervising the safety of foods, dietary supplements, drugs, vaccines, biological medical products, blood products, medical devices, radiation-emitting devices, veterinary products, and cosmetics. The FDA also enforces section 361 of the Public Health Service Act and the associated regulations, including sanitation requirements on interstate travel as well as specific rules for control of disease on products ranging from pet turtles to semen donations for assisted reproductive medicine techniques.

The FDA is an agency within the United States Department of Health and Human Services responsible for protecting and promoting the nation's public health.

a. Food and Drug Administration
b. Power III
c. 6-3-5 Brainwriting
d. 180SearchAssistant

Chapter 15. Questionnaire Design

1. A _____ is a research instrument consisting of a series of questions and other prompts for the purpose of gathering information from respondents. Although they are often designed for statistical analysis of the responses, this is not always the case. The _____ was invented by Sir Francis Galton.
   a. Market research
   b. Mystery shoppers
   c. Mystery shopping
   d. Questionnaire

2. In probability theory and statistics, _____ indicates the strength and direction of a linear relationship between two random variables. That is in contrast with the usage of the term in colloquial speech, denoting any relationship, not necessarily linear. In general statistical usage, _____ or co-relation refers to the departure of two random variables from independence.
   a. Frequency distribution
   b. Probability
   c. Mean
   d. Correlation

3. A _____ is a structured collection of records or data that is stored in a computer system. The structure is achieved by organizing the data according to a _____ model. The model in most common use today is the relational model.
   a. 6-3-5 Brainwriting
   b. 180SearchAssistant
   c. Power III
   d. Database

4. _____ is a measure of the strength of a brand, product, service relative to competitive offerings. There is often a geographic element to the competitive landscape. In defining _____, you must see to what extent a product, brand, or firm controls a product category in a given geographic area.
   a. Market dominance
   b. Productivity
   c. Discretionary spending
   d. Market system

5. In common law systems that rely on testimony by witnesses, a _____ is a question that suggests the answer or contains the information the examiner is looking for. For example, this question is leading:

   - You were at Duffy's bar on the night of July 15, weren't you?

It suggests that the witness was at Duffy's bar on the night in question. The same question in a non-leading form would be:

   - Where were you on the night of July 15?

This form of question does not suggest to the witness the answer the examiner hopes to elicit.

_____s may often be answerable with a yes or no (though not all yes-no questions are leading), while non-_____s are open-ended. Depending on the circumstances _____s can be objectionable or proper.

   a. Contract price
   b. Leading question
   c. Power III
   d. Substantive law

6. _____ is an advertisement in which a particular product specifically mentions a competitor by name for the express purpose of showing why the competitor is inferior to the product naming it.

Chapter 15. Questionnaire Design

This should not be confused with parody advertisements, where a fictional product is being advertised for the purpose of poking fun at the particular advertisement, nor should it be confused with the use of a coined brand name for the purpose of comparing the product without actually naming an actual competitor. ('Wikipedia tastes better and is less filling than the Encyclopedia Galactica.')

In the 1980s, during what has been referred to as the cola wars, soft-drink manufacturer Pepsi ran a series of advertisements where people, caught on hidden camera, in a blind taste test, chose Pepsi over rival Coca-Cola.

a. Heavy-up
b. Cost per conversion
c. Comparative advertising
d. GL-70

7. In statistics, analysis of variance (_____) is a collection of statistical models, and their associated procedures, in which the observed variance is partitioned into components due to different explanatory variables. In its simplest form _____ gives a statistical test of whether the means of several groups are all equal, and therefore generalizes Student's two-sample t-test to more than two groups.

There are three conceptual classes of such models:

1. Fixed-effects models assumes that the data came from normal populations which may differ only in their means. (Model 1)
2. Random effects models assume that the data describe a hierarchy of different populations whose differences are constrained by the hierarchy. (Model 2)
3. Mixed-effect models describe situations where both fixed and random effects are present. (Model 3)

In practice, there are several types of _____ depending on the number of treatments and the way they are applied to the subjects in the experiment:

- One-way _____ is used to test for differences among two or more independent groups. Typically, however, the one-way _____ is used to test for differences among at least three groups, since the two-group case can be covered by a T-test (Gossett, 1908.)

a. AMAX
b. ACNielsen
c. ANOVA
d. ADTECH

8. A _____ is a relatively new executive level position at a corporation, company, organization typically reporting directly to the CEO or board of directors. The _____ is responsible for a brand's image, experience, and promise, and propagating it throughout all aspects of the company. The brand officer oversees marketing, advertising, design, public relations and customer service departments.

a. Chief executive officer
b. Financial analyst
c. Power III
d. Chief brand officer

9. _____ is a computer program used for statistical analysis.

_____ (originally, Statistical Package for the Social Sciences) was released in its first version in 1968 after being founded by Norman Nie and C. Hadlai Hull. Nie was then a political science postgraduate at Stanford University, and now Research Professor in the Department of Political Science at Stanford and Professor Emeritus of Political Science at the University of Chicago.

a. 180SearchAssistant
b. 6-3-5 Brainwriting
c. Power III
d. SPSS

10. _____ is that part of statistical practice concerned with the selection of individual observations intended to yield some knowledge about a population of concern, especially for the purposes of statistical inference. Each observation measures one or more properties (weight, location, etc.) of an observable entity enumerated to distinguish objects or individuals.

a. AStore
b. Sports Marketing Group
c. Sampling
d. Richard Buckminster 'Bucky' Fuller

11. _____ is a standard point of view or personal prejudice. especially when the tendency interferes with the ability to be impartial, unprejudiced, or objective. The term _____ed is used to describe an action, judgment, or other outcome influenced by a prejudged perspective.

a. Power III
b. Bias
c. 6-3-5 Brainwriting
d. 180SearchAssistant

12. The _____ is a global navigation satellite system (GNSS) developed by the United States Department of Defense and managed by the United States Air Force 50th Space Wing. It is the only fully functional GNSS in the world, can be used freely, and is often used by civilians for navigation purposes. It uses a constellation of between 24 and 32 Medium Earth Orbit satellites that transmit precise microwave signals, which allow _____ receivers to determine their current location, the time, and their velocity.

a. 6-3-5 Brainwriting
b. 180SearchAssistant
c. Power III
d. Global positioning system

13. The business terms _____ and pull originated in the logistic and supply chain management, but are also widely used in marketing.

A _____-pull-system in business describes the move of a product or information between two subjects. On markets the consumers usually 'pulls' the goods or information they demand for their needs, while the offerers or suppliers '_____es' them toward the consumers.

a. Completely randomized designs
b. Manufacturers' representatives
c. Gold Key Matching Service
d. Push

14. _____ are a form of online advertising on the World Wide Web intended to attract web traffic or capture email addresses. It works when certain web sites open a new web browser window to display advertisements. The pop-up window containing an advertisement is usually generated by JavaScript, but can be generated by other means as well.

a. Pop-up ads
b. Power III
c. Project Portfolio Management
d. Customer intelligence

Chapter 15. Questionnaire Design

15. The U.S. _____ is an agency of the United States Department of Health and Human Services and is responsible for regulating and supervising the safety of foods, dietary supplements, drugs, vaccines, biological medical products, blood products, medical devices, radiation-emitting devices, veterinary products, and cosmetics. The FDA also enforces section 361 of the Public Health Service Act and the associated regulations, including sanitation requirements on interstate travel as well as specific rules for control of disease on products ranging from pet turtles to semen donations for assisted reproductive medicine techniques.

The FDA is an agency within the United States Department of Health and Human Services responsible for protecting and promoting the nation's public health.

   a. 6-3-5 Brainwriting
   b. Power III
   c. 180SearchAssistant
   d. Food and Drug Administration

16. Human beings are also considered to be _____ because they have the ability to change raw materials into valuable _____. The term Human _____ can also be defined as the skills, energies, talents, abilities and knowledge that are used for the production of goods or the rendering of services. While taking into account human beings as _____, the following things have to be kept in mind:

   - The size of the population
   - The capabilities of the individuals in that population

Many _____ cannot be consumed in their original form. They have to be processed in order to change them into more usable commodities.

   a. Power III
   b. 6-3-5 Brainwriting
   c. 180SearchAssistant
   d. Resources

17. _____s are used in open sentences. For instance, in the formula x + 1 = 5, x is a _____ which represents an 'unknown' number. _____s are often represented by letters of the Roman alphabet, or those of other alphabets, such as Greek, and use other special symbols.
   a. Variable
   b. Book of business
   c. Personalization
   d. Quantitative

18. _____ is a broad label that refers to any individuals or households that use goods and services generated within the economy. The concept of a _____ is used in different contexts, so that the usage and significance of the term may vary.

A _____ is a person who uses any product or service.

   a. 180SearchAssistant
   b. 6-3-5 Brainwriting
   c. Power III
   d. Consumer

19. _____ is a mathematical science pertaining to the collection, analysis, interpretation or explanation, and presentation of data. It also provides tools for prediction and forecasting based on data. It is applicable to a wide variety of academic disciplines, from the natural and social sciences to the humanities, government and business.

a. Median	b. Statistics
c. Type I error	d. Null hypothesis

20. _____ is a form of communication that typically attempts to persuade potential customers to purchase or to consume more of a particular brand of product or service. 'While now central to the contemporary global economy and the reproduction of global production networks, it is only quite recently that _____ has been more than a marginal influence on patterns of sales and production. The formation of modern _____ was intimately bound up with the emergence of new forms of monopoly capitalism around the end of the 19th and beginning of the 20th century as one element in corporate strategies to create, organize and where possible control markets, especially for mass produced consumer goods.

a. AMAX	b. ADTECH
c. ACNielsen	d. Advertising

21. Procter is a surname, and may also refer to:

- Bryan Waller Procter (pseud. Barry Cornwall), English poet
- Goodwin Procter, American law firm
- _____, consumer products multinational

a. Procter ' Gamble	b. Convergent
c. Black PRies	d. Flyer

22. _____ is the state or fact of exclusive rights and control over property, which may be an object, land/real estate, or some other kind of property (like government-granted monopolies collectively referred to as intellectual property.) It is embodied in an _____ right also referred to as title.

_____ is the key building block in the development of the capitalist socio-economic system.

a. Ownership	b. AMAX
c. ACNielsen	d. ADTECH

23. A supply chain is the system of organizations, people, technology, activities, information and resources involved in moving a product or service from _____ to customer. Supply chain activities transform natural resources, raw materials and components into a finished product that is delivered to the end customer. In sophisticated supply chain systems, used products may re-enter the supply chain at any point where residual value is recyclable.

a. Rebate	b. Bringin' Home the Oil
c. Product line extension	d. Supplier

24. In environmental modeling and especially in hydrology, a _____ model means a model that is acceptably consistent with observed natural processes, i.e. that simulates well, for example, observed river discharge. It is a key concept of the so-called Generalized Likelihood Uncertainty Estimation (GLUE) methodology to quantify how uncertain environmental predictions are.

a. 180SearchAssistant	b. 6-3-5 Brainwriting
c. Power III	d. Behavioral

25. _____ or _____ data refers to selected population characteristics as used in government, marketing or opinion research, or the _____ profiles used in such research. Note the distinction from the term 'demography' Commonly-used _____ include race, age, income, disabilities, mobility (in terms of travel time to work or number of vehicles available), educational attainment, home ownership, employment status, and even location.
- a. Albert Einstein
- b. African Americans
- c. AStore
- d. Demographic

Chapter 16. Sampling Designs and Sampling Procedures

1. A personal and cultural _____ is a relative ethic _____, an assumption upon which implementation can be extrapolated. A _____ system is a set of consistent _____s and measures that is soo not true. A principle _____ is a foundation upon which other _____s and measures of integrity are based.
   a. Package-on-Package
   b. Supreme Court of the United States
   c. Perceptual maps
   d. Value

2. A _____ is a structured collection of records or data that is stored in a computer system. The structure is achieved by organizing the data according to a _____ model. The model in most common use today is the relational model.
   a. Database
   b. 180SearchAssistant
   c. 6-3-5 Brainwriting
   d. Power III

3. _____ is that part of statistical practice concerned with the selection of individual observations intended to yield some knowledge about a population of concern, especially for the purposes of statistical inference. Each observation measures one or more properties (weight, location, etc.) of an observable entity enumerated to distinguish objects or individuals.
   a. Sports Marketing Group
   b. Richard Buckminster 'Bucky' Fuller
   c. Sampling
   d. AStore

4. A _____ is a party that mediates between a buyer and a seller. A _____ who also acts as a seller or as a buyer becomes a principal party to the deal. Distinguish agent: one who acts on behalf of a principal.
   a. Power III
   b. Spokesperson
   c. 180SearchAssistant
   d. Broker

5. _____ is an advertisement in which a particular product specifically mentions a competitor by name for the express purpose of showing why the competitor is inferior to the product naming it.

This should not be confused with parody advertisements, where a fictional product is being advertised for the purpose of poking fun at the particular advertisement, nor should it be confused with the use of a coined brand name for the purpose of comparing the product without actually naming an actual competitor. ('Wikipedia tastes better and is less filling than the Encyclopedia Galactica.')

In the 1980s, during what has been referred to as the cola wars, soft-drink manufacturer Pepsi ran a series of advertisements where people, caught on hidden camera, in a blind taste test, chose Pepsi over rival Coca-Cola.

   a. Cost per conversion
   b. Comparative advertising
   c. Heavy-up
   d. GL-70

6. In statistics, _____ or estimation error is the error caused by observing a sample instead of the whole population.

An estimate of a quantity of interest, such as an average or percentage, will generally be subject to sample-to-sample variation. These variations in the possible sample values of a statistic can theoretically be expressed as _____s, although in practice the exact _____ is typically unknown.

   a. Two-tailed test
   b. Sampling error
   c. Power III
   d. Varimax rotation

Chapter 16. Sampling Designs and Sampling Procedures

7. _____ is a statistical method involving the selection of elements from an ordered sampling frame. The most common form of _____ is an equal-probability method, in which every k^{th} element in the frame is selected, where k, the sampling interval (sometimes known as the 'skip'), is calculated as:

sample size (n) = population size (N) /k

Using this procedure each element in the population has a known and equal probability of selection. This makes _____ functionally similar to simple random sampling.

a. Selection bias
b. Systematic sampling
c. 180SearchAssistant
d. Power III

8. _____ is a broad label that refers to any individuals or households that use goods and services generated within the economy. The concept of a _____ is used in different contexts, so that the usage and significance of the term may vary.

A _____ is a person who uses any product or service.

a. 6-3-5 Brainwriting
b. Power III
c. 180SearchAssistant
d. Consumer

9. _____ is anything that is intended to save time, energy or frustration. A _____ store at a petrol station, for example, sells items that have nothing to do with gasoline/petrol, but it saves the consumer from having to go to a grocery store. '_____' is a very relative term and its meaning tends to change over time.

a. Convenience
b. Demographic profile
c. Marketing buzz
d. MaxDiff

10. _____ is a type of nonprobability sampling which involves the sample being drawn from that part of the population which is close to hand. That is, a sample population selected because it is readily available and convenient. The researcher using such a sample cannot scientifically make generalizations about the total population from this sample because it would not be representative enough.

a. AMAX
b. ACNielsen
c. ADTECH
d. Accidental sampling

11. _____ refer to a collection of facts usually collected as the result of experience, observation or experiment or a set of premises. This may consist of numbers, words particularly as measurements or observations of a set of variables. _____ are often viewed as a lowest level of abstraction from which information and knowledge are derived.

a. Pearson product-moment correlation coefficient
b. Mean
c. Sample size
d. Data

12. Sampling is the use of a subset of the population to represent the whole population. Probability sampling, or random sampling, is a sampling technique in which the probability of getting any particular sample may be calculated. _____ does not meet this criterion and should be used with caution.

a. Quota sampling
b. Power III
c. Snowball sampling
d. Nonprobability sampling

Chapter 16. Sampling Designs and Sampling Procedures

13. _____ is a way of expressing knowledge or belief that an event will occur or has occurred. In mathematics the concept has been given an exact meaning in _____ theory, that is used extensively in such areas of study as mathematics, statistics, finance, gambling, science, and philosophy to draw conclusions about the likelihood of potential events and the underlying mechanics of complex systems.
   a. Data
   b. Probability
   c. Linear regression
   d. Heteroskedastic

14. _____ is a form of communication that typically attempts to persuade potential customers to purchase or to consume more of a particular brand of product or service. 'While now central to the contemporary global economy and the reproduction of global production networks, it is only quite recently that _____ has been more than a marginal influence on patterns of sales and production. The formation of modern _____ was intimately bound up with the emergence of new forms of monopoly capitalism around the end of the 19th and beginning of the 20th century as one element in corporate strategies to create, organize and where possible control markets, especially for mass produced consumer goods.
   a. ADTECH
   b. AMAX
   c. ACNielsen
   d. Advertising

15. _____ often refers to either primary or secondary research. Secondary research involves a company using information compiled from various sources, which is about a new or existing product. The advantages of secondary research are that it is relatively cheap and easily accessible.
   a. Mystery shopping
   b. Mystery shoppers
   c. Questionnaire
   d. Market Research

16. In _____, the population is first segmented into mutually exclusive sub-groups, just as in stratified sampling. Then judgment is used to select the subjects or units from each segment based on a specified proportion. For example, an interviewer may be told to sample 200 females and 300 males between the age of 45 and 60.
   a. Power III
   b. Quota sampling
   c. Snowball sampling
   d. Nonprobability sampling

17. In statistics, a simple random sample is a subset of individuals (a sample) chosen from a larger set (a population.) Each individual is chosen randomly and entirely by chance, such that each individual has the same probability of being chosen at any stage during the sampling process, and each subset of k individuals has the same probability of being chosen for the sample as any other subset of k individuals (.) This process and technique is known as _____, and should not be confused with Random Sampling.
   a. Logit analysis
   b. Simple random sampling
   c. Market analysis
   d. Focus group

18. In social science research, _____ is a technique for developing a research sample where existing study subjects recruit future subjects from among their acquaintances. Thus the sample group appears to grow like a rolling snowball. As the sample builds up, enough data is gathered to be useful for research.
   a. Nonprobability sampling
   b. Power III
   c. Quota sampling
   d. Snowball sampling

19. In statistics, _____ is a method of sampling from a population.

Chapter 16. Sampling Designs and Sampling Procedures

When sub-populations vary considerably, it is advantageous to sample each subpopulation (stratum) independently. Stratification is the process of grouping members of the population into relatively homogeneous subgroups before sampling.

a. Coefficient of variation
b. Data
c. T-test
d. Stratified sampling

20. A _____ is any statistical test for which the distribution of the test statistic under the null hypothesis can be approximated by a normal distribution. Since many test statistics are approximately normally distributed for large samples (due to the central limit theorem), many statistical tests can be performed as approximate _____s if the sample size is not too small. In addition, some statistical tests such as comparisons of means between two samples, or a comparison of the mean of one sample to a given constant, are exact _____s under certain assumptions.

a. Confounding variables
b. Sample size
c. Z-test
d. Null hypothesis

21. In statistics, analysis of variance (_____) is a collection of statistical models, and their associated procedures, in which the observed variance is partitioned into components due to different explanatory variables. In its simplest form _____ gives a statistical test of whether the means of several groups are all equal, and therefore generalizes Student's two-sample t-test to more than two groups.

There are three conceptual classes of such models:

1. Fixed-effects models assumes that the data came from normal populations which may differ only in their means. (Model 1)
2. Random effects models assume that the data describe a hierarchy of different populations whose differences are constrained by the hierarchy. (Model 2)
3. Mixed-effect models describe situations where both fixed and random effects are present. (Model 3)

In practice, there are several types of _____ depending on the number of treatments and the way they are applied to the subjects in the experiment:

- One-way _____ is used to test for differences among two or more independent groups. Typically, however, the one-way _____ is used to test for differences among at least three groups, since the two-group case can be covered by a T-test (Gossett, 1908.)

a. ADTECH
b. AMAX
c. ANOVA
d. ACNielsen

22. _____ is a sampling technique used when 'natural' groupings are evident in a statistical population. It is often used in marketing research. In this technique, the total population is divided into these groups (or clusters) and a sample of the groups is selected.

a. Cluster sampling
b. Quota sampling
c. Power III
d. Snowball sampling

23. Procter is a surname, and may also refer to:

- Bryan Waller Procter (pseud. Barry Cornwall), English poet
- Goodwin Procter, American law firm
- _____, consumer products multinational

a. Black PRies
c. Convergent
b. Flyer
d. Procter ' Gamble

Chapter 17. Determination of Sample Size: A Review of Statistical Theory

1. The _____ is a publication of the United States Census Bureau, an agency of the United States Department of Commerce. Published annually since 1878, the statistics describe social and economic conditions in the United States.

   In 1975 a two volume Historical Statistics of the United States, Colonial Times to 1970 Bicentennial Edition was published.

   a. Statistical Abstract of the United States
   b. 6-3-5 Brainwriting
   c. Power III
   d. 180SearchAssistant

2. _____ are used to describe the basic features of the data gathered from an experimental study in various ways. A _____ is distinguished from inductive statistics. They provide simple summaries about the sample and the measures.

   a. Pearson product-moment correlation coefficient
   b. Descriptive statistics
   c. Frequency distribution
   d. P-Value

3. 'Speaking generally, properties are those physical quantities which directly describe the physical attributes of the system; _____s are those combinations of the properties which suffice to determine the response of the system. Properties can have all sorts of dimensions, depending upon the system being considered; _____s are dimensionless, or have the dimension of time or its reciprocal.'

   The term can also be used in engineering contexts, however, as it is typically used in the physical sciences.

   When the terms formal _____ and actual _____ are used, they generally correspond with the definitions used in computer science.

   a. Power III
   b. Parameter
   c. 6-3-5 Brainwriting
   d. 180SearchAssistant

4. _____ is a mathematical science pertaining to the collection, analysis, interpretation or explanation, and presentation of data. It also provides tools for prediction and forecasting based on data. It is applicable to a wide variety of academic disciplines, from the natural and social sciences to the humanities, government and business.

   a. Null hypothesis
   b. Median
   c. Type I error
   d. Statistics

5. Procter is a surname, and may also refer to:

   - Bryan Waller Procter (pseud. Barry Cornwall), English poet
   - Goodwin Procter, American law firm
   - _____, consumer products multinational

   a. Black PRies
   b. Flyer
   c. Convergent
   d. Procter ' Gamble

6. In probability theory and statistics, _____ indicates the strength and direction of a linear relationship between two random variables. That is in contrast with the usage of the term in colloquial speech, denoting any relationship, not necessarily linear. In general statistical usage, _____ or co-relation refers to the departure of two random variables from independence.

a. Frequency distribution
b. Correlation
c. Mean
d. Probability

7. _____ refer to a collection of facts usually collected as the result of experience, observation or experiment or a set of premises. This may consist of numbers, words particularly as measurements or observations of a set of variables. _____ are often viewed as a lowest level of abstraction from which information and knowledge are derived.

a. Sample size
b. Data
c. Pearson product-moment correlation coefficient
d. Mean

8. _____ is one of the four elements of marketing mix. An organization or set of organizations (go-betweens) involved in the process of making a product or service available for use or consumption by a consumer or business user.

The other three parts of the marketing mix are product, pricing, and promotion.

a. Comparison-Shopping agent
b. Distribution
c. Japan Advertising Photographers' Association
d. Better Living Through Chemistry

9. In statistics, a _____ is a tabulation of the values that one or more variables take in a sample.

Univariate _____s are often presented as lists, ordered by quantity, showing the number of times each value appears. For example, if 100 people rate a five-point Likert scale assessing their agreement with a statement on a scale on which 1 denotes strong agreement and 5 strong disagreement, the _____ of their responses might look like:

This simple tabulation has two drawbacks.

a. Confidence interval
b. Statistics
c. Survey research
d. Frequency distribution

10. _____ is a way of expressing knowledge or belief that an event will occur or has occurred. In mathematics the concept has been given an exact meaning in _____ theory, that is used extensively in such areas of study as mathematics, statistics, finance, gambling, science, and philosophy to draw conclusions about the likelihood of potential events and the underlying mechanics of complex systems.

a. Heteroskedastic
b. Linear regression
c. Data
d. Probability

11. The United States _____ is the government agency that is responsible for the United States Census. It also gathers other national demographic and economic data.

a. 6-3-5 Brainwriting
b. 180SearchAssistant
c. Power III
d. Census Bureau

12. In statistics, _____ has two related meanings:

- the arithmetic _____
- the expected value of a random variable, which is also called the population _____.

Chapter 17. Determination of Sample Size: A Review of Statistical Theory

It is sometimes stated that the '_____' _____s average. This is incorrect if '_____' is taken in the specific sense of 'arithmetic _____' as there are different types of averages: the _____, median, and mode. For instance, average house prices almost always use the median value for the average. These three types of averages are all measures of locations.

a. Standard normal distribution
b. Mean
c. Heteroskedastic
d. Confidence interval

13. In probability theory and statistics, a _____ is described as the number separating the higher half of a sample, a population from the lower half. The _____ of a finite list of numbers can be found by arranging all the observations from lowest value to highest value and picking the middle one. If there is an even number of observations, the _____ is not unique, so one often takes the mean of the two middle values.

a. Median
b. Linear regression
c. Frequency distribution
d. Statistically significant

14. _____ is a computer program used for statistical analysis.

_____ (originally, Statistical Package for the Social Sciences) was released in its first version in 1968 after being founded by Norman Nie and C. Hadlai Hull. Nie was then a political science postgraduate at Stanford University, and now Research Professor in the Department of Political Science at Stanford and Professor Emeritus of Political Science at the University of Chicago.

a. SPSS
b. Power III
c. 180SearchAssistant
d. 6-3-5 Brainwriting

15. In descriptive statistics, the _____ is the length of the smallest interval which contains all the data. It is calculated by subtracting the smallest observation (sample minimum) from the greatest (sample maximum) and provides an indication of statistical dispersion.

It is measured in the same units as the data.

a. Range
b. Japan Advertising Photographers' Association
c. Personalization
d. Just-In-Case

16. In statistics, _____ is a simple measure of the variability or dispersion of a data set. A low _____ indicates that the data points tend to be very close to the same value (the mean), while high _____ indicates that the data are 'spread out' over a large range of values.

For example, the average height for adult men in the United States is about 70 inches, with a _____ of around 3 inches.

a. Pearson product-moment correlation coefficient
b. Z-test
c. Statistically significant
d. Standard deviation

Chapter 17. Determination of Sample Size: A Review of Statistical Theory

17. In probability theory and statistics, the _____ of a random variable, probability distribution, or sample is a measure of statistical dispersion, averaging the squared distance of its possible values from the expected value (mean.) Whereas the mean is a way to describe the location of a distribution, the _____ is a way to capture its scale or degree of being spread out. The unit of _____ is the square of the unit of the original variable.

   a. Variance
   b. Standard deviation
   c. Sample size
   d. Correlation

18. _____ is that part of statistical practice concerned with the selection of individual observations intended to yield some knowledge about a population of concern, especially for the purposes of statistical inference. Each observation measures one or more properties (weight, location, etc.) of an observable entity enumerated to distinguish objects or individuals.

   a. AStore
   b. Richard Buckminster 'Bucky' Fuller
   c. Sports Marketing Group
   d. Sampling

19. In mathematics and statistics, the arithmetic mean (or simply the mean) of a list of numbers is the sum of all of the list divided by the number of items in the list. If the list is a statistical population, then the mean of that population is called a population mean. If the list is a statistical sample, we call the resulting statistic a _____.

   a. Z-test
   b. Null hypothesis
   c. Coefficient of variation
   d. Sample mean

20. The _____ of a statistical sample is the number of observations that constitute it. It is typically denoted n, a positive integer (natural number.)

Typically, all else being equal, a larger _____ leads to increased precision in estimates of various properties of the population.

   a. Data
   b. Sample size
   c. Frequency distribution
   d. Heteroskedastic

21. _____ or statistical induction comprises the use of statistics to make inferences concerning some unknown aspect of a population. It is distinguished from descriptive statistics.

Two schools of _____ are frequency probability and Bayesian inference.

   a. Probability sampling
   b. Moving average
   c. Statistical inference
   d. Standard score

22. In environmental modeling and especially in hydrology, a _____ model means a model that is acceptably consistent with observed natural processes, i.e. that simulates well, for example, observed river discharge. It is a key concept of the so-called Generalized Likelihood Uncertainty Estimation (GLUE) methodology to quantify how uncertain environmental predictions are.

   a. 180SearchAssistant
   b. Behavioral
   c. Power III
   d. 6-3-5 Brainwriting

Chapter 17. Determination of Sample Size: A Review of Statistical Theory

23. _____ is a telephone surveying technique in which the interviewer follows a script provided by a software application. The software is able to customize the flow of the questionnaire based on the answers provided, as well as information already known about the participant.

CATI may function in the following manner

- A computerized questionnaire is administered to respondents over the telephone.
- The interviewer sits in front of a computer screen
- Upon command, the computer dials the telephone number to be called.
- When contact is made, the interviewer reads the questions posed on the computer screen and records the respondent's answers directly into the computer.
- Interim and update reports can be compiled instantaneously, as the data are being collected.
- CATI software has built-in logic, which also enhances data accuracy.
- The program will personalize questions and control for logically incorrect answers, such as percentage answers that do not add up to 100 percent.
- The software has built-in branching logic, which will skip questions that are not applicable or will probe for more detail when warranted.

a. 6-3-5 Brainwriting
b. 180SearchAssistant
c. Power III
d. Computer-assisted telephone interviewing

24. In statistics, a _____ is an interval estimate of a population parameter. Instead of estimating the parameter by a single value, an interval likely to include the parameter is given. Thus, _____s are used to indicate the reliability of an estimate.
a. Confidence interval
b. T-test
c. Sample mean
d. Linear regression

25. _____s are errors in measurement that lead to measured values being inconsistent when repeated measures of a constant attribute or quantity are taken. The word random indicates that they are inherently unpredictable, and have null expected value, namely, they are scattered about the true value, and tend to have null arithmetic mean when a measurement is repeated several times with the same instrument. All measurements are prone to _____.
a. 180SearchAssistant
b. Power III
c. Systematic error
d. Random error

26. In statistics, _____ or estimation error is the error caused by observing a sample instead of the whole population.

An estimate of a quantity of interest, such as an average or percentage, will generally be subject to sample-to-sample variation. These variations in the possible sample values of a statistic can theoretically be expressed as _____s, although in practice the exact _____ is typically unknown.

a. Varimax rotation
b. Two-tailed test
c. Power III
d. Sampling error

Chapter 17. Determination of Sample Size: A Review of Statistical Theory

27. _____ is an advertisement in which a particular product specifically mentions a competitor by name for the express purpose of showing why the competitor is inferior to the product naming it.

This should not be confused with parody advertisements, where a fictional product is being advertised for the purpose of poking fun at the particular advertisement, nor should it be confused with the use of a coined brand name for the purpose of comparing the product without actually naming an actual competitor. ('Wikipedia tastes better and is less filling than the Encyclopedia Galactica.')

In the 1980s, during what has been referred to as the cola wars, soft-drink manufacturer Pepsi ran a series of advertisements where people, caught on hidden camera, in a blind taste test, chose Pepsi over rival Coca-Cola.

- a. Cost per conversion
- b. GL-70
- c. Heavy-up
- d. Comparative advertising

28. In population genetics and population ecology, _____ is the number of individual organisms in a population.

The effective _____ (N_e) is defined as 'the number of breeding individuals in an idealized population that would show the same amount of dispersion of allele frequencies under random genetic drift or the same amount of inbreeding as the population under consideration.' N_e is usually less than N (the absolute _____) and this has important applications in conservation genetics.

Small _____ results in increased genetic drift.

- a. Power III
- b. Population size
- c. 6-3-5 Brainwriting
- d. 180SearchAssistant

29. _____ is a form of communication that typically attempts to persuade potential customers to purchase or to consume more of a particular brand of product or service. 'While now central to the contemporary global economy and the reproduction of global production networks, it is only quite recently that _____ has been more than a marginal influence on patterns of sales and production. The formation of modern _____ was intimately bound up with the emergence of new forms of monopoly capitalism around the end of the 19th and beginning of the 20th century as one element in corporate strategies to create, organize and where possible control markets, especially for mass produced consumer goods.

- a. Advertising
- b. AMAX
- c. ACNielsen
- d. ADTECH

30. _____ often refers to either primary or secondary research. Secondary research involves a company using information compiled from various sources, which is about a new or existing product. The advantages of secondary research are that it is relatively cheap and easily accessible.

- a. Questionnaire
- b. Mystery shoppers
- c. Market Research
- d. Mystery shopping

31. In statistics, _____ is a method of sampling from a population.

When sub-populations vary considerably, it is advantageous to sample each subpopulation (stratum) independently. Stratification is the process of grouping members of the population into relatively homogeneous subgroups before sampling.

a. Data
b. Coefficient of variation
c. T-test
d. Stratified sampling

Chapter 18. Fieldwork

1. The United States _____ is the government agency that is responsible for the United States Census. It also gathers other national demographic and economic data.
    a. Census Bureau
    b. Power III
    c. 6-3-5 Brainwriting
    d. 180SearchAssistant

2. The _____ is a global navigation satellite system (GNSS) developed by the United States Department of Defense and managed by the United States Air Force 50th Space Wing. It is the only fully functional GNSS in the world, can be used freely, and is often used by civilians for navigation purposes. It uses a constellation of between 24 and 32 Medium Earth Orbit satellites that transmit precise microwave signals, which allow _____ receivers to determine their current location, the time, and their velocity.
    a. Power III
    b. 180SearchAssistant
    c. 6-3-5 Brainwriting
    d. Global positioning system

3. _____ is an advertisement in which a particular product specifically mentions a competitor by name for the express purpose of showing why the competitor is inferior to the product naming it.

    This should not be confused with parody advertisements, where a fictional product is being advertised for the purpose of poking fun at the particular advertisement, nor should it be confused with the use of a coined brand name for the purpose of comparing the product without actually naming an actual competitor. ('Wikipedia tastes better and is less filling than the Encyclopedia Galactica.')

    In the 1980s, during what has been referred to as the cola wars, soft-drink manufacturer Pepsi ran a series of advertisements where people, caught on hidden camera, in a blind taste test, chose Pepsi over rival Coca-Cola.

    a. Heavy-up
    b. GL-70
    c. Comparative advertising
    d. Cost per conversion

4. Human beings are also considered to be _____ because they have the ability to change raw materials into valuable _____. The term Human _____ can also be defined as the skills, energies, talents, abilities and knowledge that are used for the production of goods or the rendering of services. While taking into account human beings as _____, the following things have to be kept in mind:

    - The size of the population
    - The capabilities of the individuals in that population

    Many _____ cannot be consumed in their original form. They have to be processed in order to change them into more usable commodities.

    a. 180SearchAssistant
    b. 6-3-5 Brainwriting
    c. Power III
    d. Resources

5. In probability theory and statistics, _____ indicates the strength and direction of a linear relationship between two random variables. That is in contrast with the usage of the term in colloquial speech, denoting any relationship, not necessarily linear. In general statistical usage, _____ or co-relation refers to the departure of two random variables from independence.

Chapter 18. Fieldwork

a. Correlation
b. Mean
c. Probability
d. Frequency distribution

6. _____ refers to the production of some commodity or service, such as a television program, using a company's own funds, staff, or resources.

This is in contrast to production being outsourced (contracted out) to another company.

- Proprietary

a. Outsourcing
b. Intangible assets
c. ACNielsen
d. In-house

7. The U.S. _____ is an agency of the United States Department of Health and Human Services and is responsible for regulating and supervising the safety of foods, dietary supplements, drugs, vaccines, biological medical products, blood products, medical devices, radiation-emitting devices, veterinary products, and cosmetics. The FDA also enforces section 361 of the Public Health Service Act and the associated regulations, including sanitation requirements on interstate travel as well as specific rules for control of disease on products ranging from pet turtles to semen donations for assisted reproductive medicine techniques.

The FDA is an agency within the United States Department of Health and Human Services responsible for protecting and promoting the nation's public health.

a. Food and Drug Administration
b. 6-3-5 Brainwriting
c. Power III
d. 180SearchAssistant

8. In statistics, analysis of variance (_____) is a collection of statistical models, and their associated procedures, in which the observed variance is partitioned into components due to different explanatory variables. In its simplest form _____ gives a statistical test of whether the means of several groups are all equal, and therefore generalizes Student's two-sample t-test to more than two groups.

There are three conceptual classes of such models:

1. Fixed-effects models assumes that the data came from normal populations which may differ only in their means. (Model 1)
2. Random effects models assume that the data describe a hierarchy of different populations whose differences are constrained by the hierarchy. (Model 2)
3. Mixed-effect models describe situations where both fixed and random effects are present. (Model 3)

In practice, there are several types of _____ depending on the number of treatments and the way they are applied to the subjects in the experiment:

- One-way _____ is used to test for differences among two or more independent groups. Typically, however, the one-way _____ is used to test for differences among at least three groups, since the two-group case can be covered by a T-test (Gossett, 1908.)

a. AMAX
b. ADTECH
c. ACNielsen
d. ANOVA

9. A _____ is a research instrument consisting of a series of questions and other prompts for the purpose of gathering information from respondents. Although they are often designed for statistical analysis of the responses, this is not always the case. The _____ was invented by Sir Francis Galton.
   a. Mystery shopping
   b. Market research
   c. Mystery shoppers
   d. Questionnaire

10. _____ refer to a collection of facts usually collected as the result of experience, observation or experiment or a set of premises. This may consist of numbers, words particularly as measurements or observations of a set of variables. _____ are often viewed as a lowest level of abstraction from which information and knowledge are derived.
    a. Mean
    b. Pearson product-moment correlation coefficient
    c. Sample size
    d. Data

11. _____ is a mathematical science pertaining to the collection, analysis, interpretation or explanation, and presentation of data. It also provides tools for prediction and forecasting based on data. It is applicable to a wide variety of academic disciplines, from the natural and social sciences to the humanities, government and business.
    a. Type I error
    b. Null hypothesis
    c. Median
    d. Statistics

12. _____ is a measure of the strength of a brand, product, service relative to competitive offerings. There is often a geographic element to the competitive landscape. In defining _____, you must see to what extent a product, brand, or firm controls a product category in a given geographic area.
    a. Market system
    b. Productivity
    c. Discretionary spending
    d. Market dominance

13. _____ is a business management strategy aimed at embedding awareness of quality in all organizational processes. _____ has been widely used in manufacturing, education, call centers, government, and service industries, as well as NASA space and science programs.

When used together as a phrase, the three words in this expression have the following meanings:

- Total: Involving the entire organization, supply chain, and/or product life cycle
- Quality: With its usual definitions, with all its complexities
- Management: The system of managing with steps like Plan, Organize, Control, Lead, Staff, provisioning and organizing.

As defined by the International Organization for Standardization (ISO):

'_____ is a management approach for an organization, centered on quality, based on the participation of all its members and aiming at long-term success through customer satisfaction, and benefits to all members of the organization and to society.' ISO 8402:1994

One major aim is to reduce variation from every process so that greater consistency of effort is obtained. (Royse, D., Thyer, B., Padgett D., ' Logan T., 2006)

In Japan, _____ comprises four process steps, namely:

1. Kaizen - Focuses on 'Continuous Process Improvement', to make processes visible, repeatable and measurable.
2. Atarimae Hinshitsu - The idea that 'things will work as they are supposed to' .
3. Kansei - Examining the way the user applies the product leads to improvement in the product itself.
4. Miryokuteki Hinshitsu - The idea that 'things should have an aesthetic quality' (for example, a pen will write in a way that is pleasing to the writer.)

_____ requires that the company maintain this quality standard in all aspects of its business. This requires ensuring that things are done right the first time and that defects and waste are eliminated from operations.

a. Total quality management
c. Power III
b. 6-3-5 Brainwriting
d. 180SearchAssistant

Chapter 19. Editing and Coding: Transforming Raw Data into Information

1. Human beings are also considered to be _____ because they have the ability to change raw materials into valuable _____. The term Human _____ can also be defined as the skills, energies, talents, abilities and knowledge that are used for the production of goods or the rendering of services. While taking into account human beings as _____, the following things have to be kept in mind:

   - The size of the population
   - The capabilities of the individuals in that population

   Many _____ cannot be consumed in their original form. They have to be processed in order to change them into more usable commodities.

   a. Resources
   b. 180SearchAssistant
   c. Power III
   d. 6-3-5 Brainwriting

2. _____ refer to a collection of facts usually collected as the result of experience, observation or experiment or a set of premises. This may consist of numbers, words particularly as measurements or observations of a set of variables. _____ are often viewed as a lowest level of abstraction from which information and knowledge are derived.

   a. Sample size
   b. Pearson product-moment correlation coefficient
   c. Mean
   d. Data

3. _____ is a process of gathering, modeling, and transforming data with the goal of highlighting useful information, suggesting conclusions, and supporting decision making. _____ has multiple facets and approaches, encompassing diverse techniques under a variety of names, in different business, science, and social science domains.

   Data mining is a particular _____ technique that focuses on modeling and knowledge discovery for predictive rather than purely descriptive purposes.

   a. 180SearchAssistant
   b. 6-3-5 Brainwriting
   c. Power III
   d. Data analysis

4. _____ is a term for unprocessed data, it is also known as primary data. It is a relative term _____ can be input to a computer program or used in manual analysis procedures such as gathering statistics from a survey.

   a. Chief marketing officer
   b. Shoppers Food ' Pharmacy
   c. Product manager
   d. Raw data

5. Combining Existing _____ Sources with New Primary Data Sources

Imagine that we could get hold of a good collection of surveys taken in earlier years, such as detailed studies about changes going on in this phase and hopefully additional studies in the years to come. Analyzing this data base over time could give us a good picture of what changes actually have taken place in the orientation of the population and of the extent to which new technical concepts did have an impact on subgroups of the population. Furthermore, data archives can help to prepare studies on change over time by monitoring what questions have been asked in earlier years and alerting principal investigators to important questions which should be repeated in planned research projects.

Chapter 19. Editing and Coding: Transforming Raw Data into Information

a. 6-3-5 Brainwriting
b. 180SearchAssistant
c. Power III
d. Secondary data

6. _____ is a telephone surveying technique in which the interviewer follows a script provided by a software application. The software is able to customize the flow of the questionnaire based on the answers provided, as well as information already known about the participant.

CATI may function in the following manner

- A computerized questionnaire is administered to respondents over the telephone.
- The interviewer sits in front of a computer screen
- Upon command, the computer dials the telephone number to be called.
- When contact is made, the interviewer reads the questions posed on the computer screen and records the respondent's answers directly into the computer.
- Interim and update reports can be compiled instantaneously, as the data are being collected.
- CATI software has built-in logic, which also enhances data accuracy.
- The program will personalize questions and control for logically incorrect answers, such as percentage answers that do not add up to 100 percent.
- The software has built-in branching logic, which will skip questions that are not applicable or will probe for more detail when warranted.

a. 180SearchAssistant
b. 6-3-5 Brainwriting
c. Power III
d. Computer-assisted telephone interviewing

7. _____ refers to the production of some commodity or service, such as a television program, using a company's own funds, staff, or resources.

This is in contrast to production being outsourced (contracted out) to another company.

- Proprietary

a. Outsourcing
b. Intangible assets
c. ACNielsen
d. In-house

8. In probability theory and statistics, _____ indicates the strength and direction of a linear relationship between two random variables. That is in contrast with the usage of the term in colloquial speech, denoting any relationship, not necessarily linear. In general statistical usage, _____ or co-relation refers to the departure of two random variables from independence.

a. Mean
b. Frequency distribution
c. Correlation
d. Probability

Chapter 19. Editing and Coding: Transforming Raw Data into Information

9. A personal and cultural _____ is a relative ethic _____, an assumption upon which implementation can be extrapolated. A _____ system is a set of consistent _____s and measures that is soo not true. A principle _____ is a foundation upon which other _____s and measures of integrity are based.
   a. Package-on-Package
   b. Supreme Court of the United States
   c. Perceptual maps
   d. Value

10. A _____ is a research instrument consisting of a series of questions and other prompts for the purpose of gathering information from respondents. Although they are often designed for statistical analysis of the responses, this is not always the case. The _____ was invented by Sir Francis Galton.
    a. Questionnaire
    b. Mystery shoppers
    c. Mystery shopping
    d. Market research

11. An _____ is a special-purpose computer system designed to perform one or a few dedicated functions, often with real-time computing constraints. It is usually embedded as part of a complete device including hardware and mechanical parts. In contrast, a general-purpose computer, such as a personal computer, can do many different tasks depending on programming.
    a. ADTECH
    b. ACNielsen
    c. AMAX
    d. Embedded system

Chapter 20. Basic Data Analysis: Descriptive Statistics

1. The _____ is a publication of the United States Census Bureau, an agency of the United States Department of Commerce. Published annually since 1878, the statistics describe social and economic conditions in the United States.

In 1975 a two volume Historical Statistics of the United States, Colonial Times to 1970 Bicentennial Edition was published.

   a. 6-3-5 Brainwriting
   b. 180SearchAssistant
   c. Power III
   d. Statistical Abstract of the United States

2. _____ is a broad label that refers to any individuals or households that use goods and services generated within the economy. The concept of a _____ is used in different contexts, so that the usage and significance of the term may vary.

A _____ is a person who uses any product or service.

   a. 6-3-5 Brainwriting
   b. Consumer
   c. Power III
   d. 180SearchAssistant

3. In probability theory and statistics, _____ indicates the strength and direction of a linear relationship between two random variables. That is in contrast with the usage of the term in colloquial speech, denoting any relationship, not necessarily linear. In general statistical usage, _____ or co-relation refers to the departure of two random variables from independence.
   a. Frequency distribution
   b. Correlation
   c. Mean
   d. Probability

4. The _____ is a professional association for marketers. As of 2008 it had approximately 40,000 members. There are collegiate chapters on 250 campuses.
   a. ACNielsen
   b. ADTECH
   c. AMAX
   d. American Marketing Association

5. _____ is a branch of philosophy which seeks to address questions about morality, such as how a moral outcome can be achieved in a specific situation (applied _____), how moral values should be determined (normative _____), what moral values people actually abide by (descriptive _____), what the fundamental semantic, ontological, and epistemic nature of _____ or morality is (meta-_____), and how moral capacity or moral agency develops and what its nature is (moral psychology.)

Socrates was one of the first Greek philosophers to encourage both scholars and the common citizen to turn their attention from the outside world to the condition of man. In this view, Knowledge having a bearing on human life was placed highest, all other knowledge being secondary.

   a. ADTECH
   b. ACNielsen
   c. AMAX
   d. Ethics

6. _____ is defined by the American _____ Association as the activity, set of institutions, and processes for creating, communicating, delivering, and exchanging offerings that have value for customers, clients, partners, and society at large. The term developed from the original meaning which referred literally to going to market, as in shopping, or going to a market to sell goods or services.

_____ practice tends to be seen as a creative industry, which includes advertising, distribution and selling.

a. Product naming
b. Marketing
c. Marketing myopia
d. Customer acquisition management

7. _____s are used in open sentences. For instance, in the formula x + 1 = 5, x is a _____ which represents an 'unknown' number. _____s are often represented by letters of the Roman alphabet, or those of other alphabets, such as Greek, and use other special symbols.

a. Personalization
b. Variable
c. Book of business
d. Quantitative

8. _____ refer to a collection of facts usually collected as the result of experience, observation or experiment or a set of premises. This may consist of numbers, words particularly as measurements or observations of a set of variables. _____ are often viewed as a lowest level of abstraction from which information and knowledge are derived.

a. Data
b. Sample size
c. Pearson product-moment correlation coefficient
d. Mean

9. In probability theory and statistics, a _____ is described as the number separating the higher half of a sample, a population from the lower half. The _____ of a finite list of numbers can be found by arranging all the observations from lowest value to highest value and picking the middle one. If there is an even number of observations, the _____ is not unique, so one often takes the mean of the two middle values.

a. Median
b. Linear regression
c. Frequency distribution
d. Statistically significant

10. The _____ is a global navigation satellite system (GNSS) developed by the United States Department of Defense and managed by the United States Air Force 50th Space Wing. It is the only fully functional GNSS in the world, can be used freely, and is often used by civilians for navigation purposes. It uses a constellation of between 24 and 32 Medium Earth Orbit satellites that transmit precise microwave signals, which allow _____ receivers to determine their current location, the time, and their velocity.

a. 180SearchAssistant
b. 6-3-5 Brainwriting
c. Global positioning system
d. Power III

11. _____ is a computer program used for statistical analysis.

_____ (originally, Statistical Package for the Social Sciences) was released in its first version in 1968 after being founded by Norman Nie and C. Hadlai Hull. Nie was then a political science postgraduate at Stanford University,and now Research Professor in the Department of Political Science at Stanford and Professor Emeritus of Political Science at the University of Chicago.

a. Power III
b. 6-3-5 Brainwriting
c. SPSS
d. 180SearchAssistant

12. _____ is a telephone surveying technique in which the interviewer follows a script provided by a software application. The software is able to customize the flow of the questionnaire based on the answers provided, as well as information already known about the participant.

Chapter 20. Basic Data Analysis: Descriptive Statistics

CATI may function in the following manner

- A computerized questionnaire is administered to respondents over the telephone.
- The interviewer sits in front of a computer screen
- Upon command, the computer dials the telephone number to be called.
- When contact is made, the interviewer reads the questions posed on the computer screen and records the respondent's answers directly into the computer.
- Interim and update reports can be compiled instantaneously, as the data are being collected.
- CATI software has built-in logic, which also enhances data accuracy.
- The program will personalize questions and control for logically incorrect answers, such as percentage answers that do not add up to 100 percent.
- The software has built-in branching logic, which will skip questions that are not applicable or will probe for more detail when warranted.

a. 6-3-5 Brainwriting
b. 180SearchAssistant
c. Power III
d. Computer-assisted telephone interviewing

13. In descriptive statistics, the _____ is the length of the smallest interval which contains all the data. It is calculated by subtracting the smallest observation (sample minimum) from the greatest (sample maximum) and provides an indication of statistical dispersion.

It is measured in the same units as the data.

a. Personalization
b. Just-In-Case
c. Range
d. Japan Advertising Photographers' Association

Chapter 21. Univariate Statistical Analysis

1. _____ is a mathematical science pertaining to the collection, analysis, interpretation or explanation, and presentation of data. It also provides tools for prediction and forecasting based on data. It is applicable to a wide variety of academic disciplines, from the natural and social sciences to the humanities, government and business.
    a. Null hypothesis
    b. Type I error
    c. Median
    d. Statistics

2. _____ is an advertisement in which a particular product specifically mentions a competitor by name for the express purpose of showing why the competitor is inferior to the product naming it.

    This should not be confused with parody advertisements, where a fictional product is being advertised for the purpose of poking fun at the particular advertisement, nor should it be confused with the use of a coined brand name for the purpose of comparing the product without actually naming an actual competitor. ('Wikipedia tastes better and is less filling than the Encyclopedia Galactica.')

    In the 1980s, during what has been referred to as the cola wars, soft-drink manufacturer Pepsi ran a series of advertisements where people, caught on hidden camera, in a blind taste test, chose Pepsi over rival Coca-Cola.

    a. Heavy-up
    b. Cost per conversion
    c. GL-70
    d. Comparative advertising

3. The _____ is a publication of the United States Census Bureau, an agency of the United States Department of Commerce. Published annually since 1878, the statistics describe social and economic conditions in the United States.

    In 1975 a two volume Historical Statistics of the United States, Colonial Times to 1970 Bicentennial Edition was published.

    a. Power III
    b. 180SearchAssistant
    c. 6-3-5 Brainwriting
    d. Statistical Abstract of the United States

4. In statistical hypothesis testing, the _____ formally describes some aspect of the statistical behaviour of a set of data; this description is treated as valid unless the actual behaviour of the data contradicts this assumption. Thus, the _____ is contrasted against another hypothesis. Statistical hypothesis testing is used to make a decision about whether the data contradicts the _____: this is called significance testing.
    a. Standard score
    b. Null hypothesis
    c. Statistical hypothesis test
    d. Variance

5. The _____ and the null hypothesis are the two rival hypotheses whose likelihoods are compared by a statistical hypothesis test. Usually the _____ is the possibility that an observed effect is genuine and the null hypothesis is the rival possibility that it has resulted from chance.

    The classical (or frequentist) approach is to calculate the probability that the observed effect (or one more extreme) will occur if the null hypothesis is true.

    a. ACNielsen
    b. Analysis of variance
    c. Alternative hypothesis
    d. Interval estimation

Chapter 21. Univariate Statistical Analysis

6. In statistical hypothesis testing, the _____ is the probability of obtaining a result at least as extreme as the one that was actually observed, assuming that the null hypothesis is true. The fact that _____s are based on this assumption is crucial to their correct interpretation.

More technically, a _____ of an experiment is a random variable defined over the sample space of the experiment such that its distribution under the null hypothesis is uniform on the interval [0,1].

   a. Descriptive statistics
   b. Pearson product-moment correlation coefficient
   c. Correlation
   d. P-value

7. The _____ of a test is a traditional frequentist statistical hypothesis testing concept. In simple cases, it is defined as the probability of making a decision to reject the null hypothesis when the null hypothesis is actually true (a decision known as a Type I error, or 'false positive determination'.) The decision is often made using the p-value: if the p-value is less than the _____, then the null hypothesis is rejected.
   a. Standard deviation
   b. Type I error
   c. Significance level
   d. Statistical hypothesis test

8. A personal and cultural _____ is a relative ethic _____, an assumption upon which implementation can be extrapolated. A _____ system is a set of consistent _____s and measures that is soo not true. A principle _____ is a foundation upon which other _____s and measures of integrity are based.
   a. Perceptual maps
   b. Supreme Court of the United States
   c. Value
   d. Package-on-Package

9. In statistics, the terms _____ and type II error are used to describe possible errors made in a statistical decision process. In 1928, Jerzy Neyman (1894-1981) and Egon Pearson (1895-1980), both eminent statisticians, discussed the problems associated with 'deciding whether or not a particular sample may be judged as likely to have been randomly drawn from a certain population' (1928/1967, p.1): and identified 'two sources of error', namely:

   Type I (>α): reject the null-hypothesis when the null-hypothesis is true, and
   Type II (>β): fail to reject the null-hypothesis when the null-hypothesis is false

In 1930, they elaborated on these two sources of error, remarking that 'in testing hypotheses two considerations must be kept in view, (1) we must be able to reduce the chance of rejecting a true hypothesis to as low a value as desired; (2) the test must be so devised that it will reject the hypothesis tested when it is likely to be false'

Scientists recognize two different sorts of error:

- Statistical error: the difference between a computed, estimated specified and inherently unpredictable fluctuations in the measurement apparatus or the system being studied.
- Systematic error: the difference between a computed, estimated specified and which, once identified, can usually be eliminated.

Chapter 21. Univariate Statistical Analysis

Statisticians speak of two significant sorts of statistical error. The context is that there is a 'null hypothesis' which corresponds to a presumed default 'state of nature', e.g., that an individual is free of disease, that an accused is innocent that is, that the individual has the disease, that the accused is guilty, or that the login candidate is an authorized user.

   a. Significance level   b. Probability sampling
   c. Mean   d. Type I error

10. _____ refer to a collection of facts usually collected as the result of experience, observation or experiment or a set of premises. This may consist of numbers, words particularly as measurements or observations of a set of variables. _____ are often viewed as a lowest level of abstraction from which information and knowledge are derived.
   a. Sample size   b. Mean
   c. Pearson product-moment correlation coefficient   d. Data

11. _____ is a way of expressing knowledge or belief that an event will occur or has occurred. In mathematics the concept has been given an exact meaning in _____ theory, that is used extensively in such areas of study as mathematics, statistics, finance, gambling, science, and philosophy to draw conclusions about the likelihood of potential events and the underlying mechanics of complex systems.
   a. Probability   b. Data
   c. Heteroskedastic   d. Linear regression

12. _____s are used in open sentences. For instance, in the formula x + 1 = 5, x is a _____ which represents an 'unknown' number. _____s are often represented by letters of the Roman alphabet, or those of other alphabets, such as Greek, and use other special symbols.
   a. Personalization   b. Quantitative
   c. Book of business   d. Variable

13. Human beings are also considered to be _____ because they have the ability to change raw materials into valuable _____. The term Human _____ can also be defined as the skills, energies, talents, abilities and knowledge that are used for the production of goods or the rendering of services. While taking into account human beings as _____, the following things have to be kept in mind:

- The size of the population
- The capabilities of the individuals in that population

Many _____ cannot be consumed in their original form. They have to be processed in order to change them into more usable commodities.

   a. 180SearchAssistant   b. Power III
   c. 6-3-5 Brainwriting   d. Resources

14. An example of a repeated measures _____ would be if one group were pre- and post-tested. (This example occurs in education quite frequently.) If a teacher wanted to examine the effect of a new set of textbooks on student achievement, (s)he could test the class at the beginning of the year (pretest) and at the end of the year (posttest.)

Chapter 21. Univariate Statistical Analysis

a. T-test
c. Null hypothesis
b. Moving average
d. Statistically significant

15. _____ is a computer program used for statistical analysis.

_____ (originally, Statistical Package for the Social Sciences) was released in its first version in 1968 after being founded by Norman Nie and C. Hadlai Hull. Nie was then a political science postgraduate at Stanford University, and now Research Professor in the Department of Political Science at Stanford and Professor Emeritus of Political Science at the University of Chicago.

a. SPSS
c. 180SearchAssistant
b. 6-3-5 Brainwriting
d. Power III

16. _____ is a telephone surveying technique in which the interviewer follows a script provided by a software application. The software is able to customize the flow of the questionnaire based on the answers provided, as well as information already known about the participant.

CATI may function in the following manner

- A computerized questionnaire is administered to respondents over the telephone.
- The interviewer sits in front of a computer screen
- Upon command, the computer dials the telephone number to be called.
- When contact is made, the interviewer reads the questions posed on the computer screen and records the respondent's answers directly into the computer.
- Interim and update reports can be compiled instantaneously, as the data are being collected.
- CATI software has built-in logic, which also enhances data accuracy.
- The program will personalize questions and control for logically incorrect answers, such as percentage answers that do not add up to 100 percent.
- The software has built-in branching logic, which will skip questions that are not applicable or will probe for more detail when warranted.

a. Power III
c. 180SearchAssistant
b. 6-3-5 Brainwriting
d. Computer-assisted telephone interviewing

17. In statistics, a _____ is an interval estimate of a population parameter. Instead of estimating the parameter by a single value, an interval likely to include the parameter is given. Thus, _____ s are used to indicate the reliability of an estimate.

a. Sample mean
c. Linear regression
b. T-test
d. Confidence interval

18. In statistics, _____ is a simple measure of the variability or dispersion of a data set. A low _____ indicates that the data points tend to be very close to the same value (the mean), while high _____ indicates that the data are 'spread out' over a large range of values.

Chapter 21. Univariate Statistical Analysis

For example, the average height for adult men in the United States is about 70 inches, with a _____ of around 3 inches.

a. Pearson product-moment correlation coefficient
b. Statistically significant
c. Z-test
d. Standard deviation

19. The _____ is a statistical test used in inference, in which a given statistical hypothesis will be rejected when the value of the statistic is either sufficiently small or sufficiently large. The test is named after the 'tail' of data under the far left and far right of a bell-shaped normal data distribution, or bell curve. However, the terminology is extended to tests relating to distributions other than normal.
   a. Varimax rotation
   b. Sampling error
   c. Power III
   d. Two-tailed test

20. _____ is the ability of an individual or group to seclude themselves or information about themselves and thereby reveal themselves selectively. The boundaries and content of what is considered private differ among cultures and individuals, but share basic common themes. _____ is sometimes related to anonymity, the wish to remain unnoticed or unidentified in the public realm.
   a. 6-3-5 Brainwriting
   b. Power III
   c. 180SearchAssistant
   d. Privacy

21. A _____ is any statistical hypothesis test in which the test statistic has a chi-square distribution when the null hypothesis is true, or any in which the probability distribution of the test statistic (assuming the null hypothesis is true) can be made to approximate a chi-square distribution as closely as desired by making the sample size large enough.

Some examples of chi-squared tests where the chi-square distribution is only approximately valid:

- Pearson's _____, also known as the chi-square goodness-of-fit test or _____ for independence. When mentioned without any modifiers or without other precluding context, this test is usually understood.
- Yates' _____, also known as Yates' correction for continuity.
- Mantel-Haenszel _____.
- Linear-by-linear association _____.
- The portmanteau test in time-series analysis, testing for the presence of autocorrelation
- Likelihood-ratio tests in general statistical modelling, for testing whether there is evidence of the need to move from a simple model to a more complicated one (where the simple model is nested within the complicated one.)

One case where the distribution of the test statistic is an exact chi-square distribution is the test that the variance of a normally-distributed population has a given value based on a sample variance. Such a test is uncommon in practice because values of variances to test against are seldom known exactly.

If a sample of size n is taken from a population having a normal distribution, then there is a well-known result which allows a test to be made of whether the variance of the population has a pre-determined value.

Chapter 21. Univariate Statistical Analysis

a. Chi-square test
c. Type I error

b. Confounding variables
d. Randomization

22. Procter is a surname, and may also refer to:

- Bryan Waller Procter (pseud. Barry Cornwall), English poet
- Goodwin Procter, American law firm
- _____, consumer products multinational

a. Procter ' Gamble
c. Flyer

b. Black PRies
d. Convergent

Chapter 22. Bivariate Statistical Analysis: Differences Between Two Variables

1. _____ is a broad label that refers to any individuals or households that use goods and services generated within the economy. The concept of a _____ is used in different contexts, so that the usage and significance of the term may vary.

A _____ is a person who uses any product or service.

   a. 6-3-5 Brainwriting
   b. Consumer
   c. Power III
   d. 180SearchAssistant

2. _____ is the ability of an individual or group to seclude themselves or information about themselves and thereby reveal themselves selectively. The boundaries and content of what is considered private differ among cultures and individuals, but share basic common themes. _____ is sometimes related to anonymity, the wish to remain unnoticed or unidentified in the public realm.
   a. Power III
   b. 180SearchAssistant
   c. 6-3-5 Brainwriting
   d. Privacy

3. The _____ is a publication of the United States Census Bureau, an agency of the United States Department of Commerce. Published annually since 1878, the statistics describe social and economic conditions in the United States.

In 1975 a two volume Historical Statistics of the United States, Colonial Times to 1970 Bicentennial Edition was published.

   a. Power III
   b. 180SearchAssistant
   c. 6-3-5 Brainwriting
   d. Statistical Abstract of the United States

4. A _____ is any statistical hypothesis test in which the test statistic has a chi-square distribution when the null hypothesis is true, or any in which the probability distribution of the test statistic (assuming the null hypothesis is true) can be made to approximate a chi-square distribution as closely as desired by making the sample size large enough.

Some examples of chi-squared tests where the chi-square distribution is only approximately valid:

   - Pearson's _____, also known as the chi-square goodness-of-fit test or _____ for independence. When mentioned without any modifiers or without other precluding context, this test is usually understood.
   - Yates' _____, also known as Yates' correction for continuity.
   - Mantel-Haenszel _____.
   - Linear-by-linear association _____.
   - The portmanteau test in time-series analysis, testing for the presence of autocorrelation
   - Likelihood-ratio tests in general statistical modelling, for testing whether there is evidence of the need to move from a simple model to a more complicated one (where the simple model is nested within the complicated one.)

One case where the distribution of the test statistic is an exact chi-square distribution is the test that the variance of a normally-distributed population has a given value based on a sample variance. Such a test is uncommon in practice because values of variances to test against are seldom known exactly.

Chapter 22. Bivariate Statistical Analysis: Differences Between Two Variables 113

If a sample of size n is taken from a population having a normal distribution, then there is a well-known result which allows a test to be made of whether the variance of the population has a pre-determined value.

a. Randomization
b. Type I error
c. Confounding variables
d. Chi-square test

5. An example of a repeated measures _____ would be if one group were pre- and post-tested. (This example occurs in education quite frequently.) If a teacher wanted to examine the effect of a new set of textbooks on student achievement, (s)he could test the class at the beginning of the year (pretest) and at the end of the year (posttest.)
a. T-test
b. Null hypothesis
c. Moving average
d. Statistically significant

6. A _____ is any statistical test for which the distribution of the test statistic under the null hypothesis can be approximated by a normal distribution. Since many test statistics are approximately normally distributed for large samples (due to the central limit theorem), many statistical tests can be performed as approximate _____s if the sample size is not too small. In addition, some statistical tests such as comparisons of means between two samples, or a comparison of the mean of one sample to a given constant, are exact _____s under certain assumptions.
a. Null hypothesis
b. Z-test
c. Sample size
d. Confounding variables

7. The _____ is a global navigation satellite system (GNSS) developed by the United States Department of Defense and managed by the United States Air Force 50th Space Wing. It is the only fully functional GNSS in the world, can be used freely, and is often used by civilians for navigation purposes. It uses a constellation of between 24 and 32 Medium Earth Orbit satellites that transmit precise microwave signals, which allow _____ receivers to determine their current location, the time, and their velocity.
a. 180SearchAssistant
b. Power III
c. 6-3-5 Brainwriting
d. Global positioning system

8. In statistics, _____ has two related meanings:

- the arithmetic _____
- the expected value of a random variable, which is also called the population _____.

It is sometimes stated that the '_____' _____s average. This is incorrect if '_____' is taken in the specific sense of 'arithmetic _____' as there are different types of averages: the _____, median, and mode. For instance, average house prices almost always use the median value for the average. These three types of averages are all measures of locations.

a. Confidence interval
b. Standard normal distribution
c. Heteroskedastic
d. Mean

9. In probability theory and statistics, the _____ of a random variable, probability distribution, or sample is a measure of statistical dispersion, averaging the squared distance of its possible values from the expected value (mean.) Whereas the mean is a way to describe the location of a distribution, the _____ is a way to capture its scale or degree of being spread out. The unit of _____ is the square of the unit of the original variable.

a. Standard deviation
b. Sample size
c. Correlation
d. Variance

10. In statistics, analysis of variance (_____) is a collection of statistical models, and their associated procedures, in which the observed variance is partitioned into components due to different explanatory variables. In its simplest form _____ gives a statistical test of whether the means of several groups are all equal, and therefore generalizes Student's two-sample t-test to more than two groups.

There are three conceptual classes of such models:

1. Fixed-effects models assumes that the data came from normal populations which may differ only in their means. (Model 1)
2. Random effects models assume that the data describe a hierarchy of different populations whose differences are constrained by the hierarchy. (Model 2)
3. Mixed-effect models describe situations where both fixed and random effects are present. (Model 3)

In practice, there are several types of _____ depending on the number of treatments and the way they are applied to the subjects in the experiment:

- One-way _____ is used to test for differences among two or more independent groups. Typically, however, the one-way _____ is used to test for differences among at least three groups, since the two-group case can be covered by a T-test (Gossett, 1908.)

a. AMAX
b. ACNielsen
c. ANOVA
d. ADTECH

11. In statistics, _____ is a collection of statistical models, and their associated procedures, in which the observed variance is partitioned into components due to different explanatory variables. The initial techniques of the _____ were developed by the statistician and geneticist R. A. Fisher in the 1920s and 1930s, and is sometimes known as Fisher's ANOVA or Fisher's _____, due to the use of Fisher's F-distribution as part of the test of statistical significance.

There are three conceptual classes of such models:

1. Fixed-effects models assumes that the data came from normal populations which may differ only in their means. (Model 1)
2. Random effects models assume that the data describe a hierarchy of different populations whose differences are constrained by the hierarchy. (Model 2)
3. Mixed-effect models describe situations where both fixed and random effects are present. (Model 3)

In practice, there are several types of ANOVA depending on the number of treatments and the way they are applied to the subjects in the experiment:

- One-way ANOVA is used to test for differences among two or more independent groups. Typically, however, the One-way ANOVA is used to test for differences among at least three groups, since the two-group case can be covered by a T-test (Gossett, 1908.)

Chapter 22. Bivariate Statistical Analysis: Differences Between Two Variables

a. Arithmetic mean
b. ACNielsen
c. Analysis of variance
d. Interval estimation

12. _____ is that part of statistical practice concerned with the selection of individual observations intended to yield some knowledge about a population of concern, especially for the purposes of statistical inference. Each observation measures one or more properties (weight, location, etc.) of an observable entity enumerated to distinguish objects or individuals.

a. AStore
b. Sports Marketing Group
c. Richard Buckminster 'Bucky' Fuller
d. Sampling

Chapter 23. Bivariate Statistical Analysis: Measures of Association

1. The U.S. _____ is an agency of the United States Department of Health and Human Services and is responsible for regulating and supervising the safety of foods, dietary supplements, drugs, vaccines, biological medical products, blood products, medical devices, radiation-emitting devices, veterinary products, and cosmetics. The FDA also enforces section 361 of the Public Health Service Act and the associated regulations, including sanitation requirements on interstate travel as well as specific rules for control of disease on products ranging from pet turtles to semen donations for assisted reproductive medicine techniques.

The FDA is an agency within the United States Department of Health and Human Services responsible for protecting and promoting the nation's public health.

   a. Power III
   b. 6-3-5 Brainwriting
   c. 180SearchAssistant
   d. Food and Drug Administration

2. _____ is the ability of an individual or group to seclude themselves or information about themselves and thereby reveal themselves selectively. The boundaries and content of what is considered private differ among cultures and individuals, but share basic common themes. _____ is sometimes related to anonymity, the wish to remain unnoticed or unidentified in the public realm.

   a. 180SearchAssistant
   b. Privacy
   c. 6-3-5 Brainwriting
   d. Power III

3. A _____ is any statistical hypothesis test in which the test statistic has a chi-square distribution when the null hypothesis is true, or any in which the probability distribution of the test statistic (assuming the null hypothesis is true) can be made to approximate a chi-square distribution as closely as desired by making the sample size large enough.

Some examples of chi-squared tests where the chi-square distribution is only approximately valid:

- Pearson's _____, also known as the chi-square goodness-of-fit test or _____ for independence. When mentioned without any modifiers or without other precluding context, this test is usually understood.
- Yates' _____, also known as Yates' correction for continuity.
- Mantel-Haenszel _____.
- Linear-by-linear association _____.
- The portmanteau test in time-series analysis, testing for the presence of autocorrelation
- Likelihood-ratio tests in general statistical modelling, for testing whether there is evidence of the need to move from a simple model to a more complicated one (where the simple model is nested within the complicated one.)

One case where the distribution of the test statistic is an exact chi-square distribution is the test that the variance of a normally-distributed population has a given value based on a sample variance. Such a test is uncommon in practice because values of variances to test against are seldom known exactly.

If a sample of size n is taken from a population having a normal distribution, then there is a well-known result which allows a test to be made of whether the variance of the population has a pre-determined value.

a. Chi-square test
b. Type I error
c. Confounding variables
d. Randomization

4. In statistics, the _____ is a common measure of the correlation (linear dependence) between two variables X and Y. It is very widely used in the sciences as a measure of the strength of linear dependence between two variables, giving a value somewhere between +1 and -1 inclusive. It was first introduced by Francis Galton in the 1880s, and named after Karl Pearson.

In accordance with the usual convention, when calculated for an entire population, the Pearson product-moment correlation is typically designated by the analogous Greek letter, which in this case is ρ .

a. Standard deviation
b. Pearson product-moment correlation coefficient
c. Control chart
d. Median

5. In probability theory and statistics, _____ indicates the strength and direction of a linear relationship between two random variables. That is in contrast with the usage of the term in colloquial speech, denoting any relationship, not necessarily linear. In general statistical usage, _____ or co-relation refers to the departure of two random variables from independence.
a. Mean
b. Frequency distribution
c. Probability
d. Correlation

6. A personal and cultural _____ is a relative ethic _____, an assumption upon which implementation can be extrapolated. A _____ system is a set of consistent _____s and measures that is soo not true. A principle _____ is a foundation upon which other _____s and measures of integrity are based.
a. Package-on-Package
b. Value
c. Supreme Court of the United States
d. Perceptual maps

7. _____ is a telephone surveying technique in which the interviewer follows a script provided by a software application. The software is able to customize the flow of the questionnaire based on the answers provided, as well as information already known about the participant.

CATI may function in the following manner

- A computerized questionnaire is administered to respondents over the telephone.
- The interviewer sits in front of a computer screen
- Upon command, the computer dials the telephone number to be called.
- When contact is made, the interviewer reads the questions posed on the computer screen and records the respondent's answers directly into the computer.
- Interim and update reports can be compiled instantaneously, as the data are being collected.
- CATI software has built-in logic, which also enhances data accuracy.
- The program will personalize questions and control for logically incorrect answers, such as percentage answers that do not add up to 100 percent.
- The software has built-in branching logic, which will skip questions that are not applicable or will probe for more detail when warranted.

a. 180SearchAssistant
b. 6-3-5 Brainwriting
c. Computer-assisted telephone interviewing
d. Power III

8. In statistics, the _____, R^2 is used in the context of statistical models whose main purpose is the prediction of future outcomes on the basis of other related information. It is the proportion of variability in a data set that is accounted for by the statistical model. It provides a measure of how well future outcomes are likely to be predicted by the model.
   a. Coefficient of determination
   b. Multicollinearity
   c. Variance inflation factor
   d. Regression analysis

9. In statistics, _____ is used for two things;

- to construct a simple formula that will predict what value will occur for a quantity of interest when other related variables take given values.
- to allow a test to be made of whether a given variable does have an effect on a quantity of interest in situations where there may be many related variables.

In both cases, several sets of outcomes are available for the quantity of interest together with the related variables.

_____ is a form of regression analysis in which the relationship between one or more independent variables and another variable, called the dependent variable, is modelled by a least squares function, called a _____ equation. This function is a linear combination of one or more model parameters, called regression coefficients. A _____ equation with one independent variable represents a straight line when the predicted value (i.e. the dependant variable from the regression equation) is plotted against the independent variable: this is called a simple _____.

a. Sample size
b. Linear regression
c. Heteroskedastic
d. Descriptive statistics

Chapter 23. Bivariate Statistical Analysis: Measures of Association

10. 'Speaking generally, properties are those physical quantities which directly describe the physical attributes of the system; _____s are those combinations of the properties which suffice to determine the response of the system. Properties can have all sorts of dimensions, depending upon the system being considered; _____s are dimensionless, or have the dimension of time or its reciprocal.'

The term can also be used in engineering contexts, however, as it is typically used in the physical sciences.

When the terms formal _____ and actual _____ are used, they generally correspond with the definitions used in computer science.

a. 180SearchAssistant
b. Power III
c. 6-3-5 Brainwriting
d. Parameter

11. In statistics, _____ is a collective name for techniques for the modeling and analysis of numerical data consisting of values of a dependent variable and of one or more independent variables The dependent variable in the regression equation is modeled as a function of the independent variables, corresponding parameters, and an error term. The error term is treated as a random variable.

a. Multicollinearity
b. Regression analysis
c. Variance inflation factor
d. Stepwise regression

12. _____ is a computer program used for statistical analysis.

_____ (originally, Statistical Package for the Social Sciences) was released in its first version in 1968 after being founded by Norman Nie and C. Hadlai Hull. Nie was then a political science postgraduate at Stanford University,and now Research Professor in the Department of Political Science at Stanford and Professor Emeritus of Political Science at the University of Chicago.

a. 6-3-5 Brainwriting
b. 180SearchAssistant
c. Power III
d. SPSS

13. A _____ is a statement or claim that a particular event will occur in the future in more certain terms than a forecast. The etymology of this word is Latin . In regards to predicting the future Howard H. Stevenson Says, ' _____ is at least two things: Important and hard.' Important, because we have to act, and hard because we have to realize the future we want, and what is the best way to get there.

a. 6-3-5 Brainwriting
b. Prediction
c. Power III
d. 180SearchAssistant

14. In statistics, a result is called _____ if it is unlikely to have occurred by chance. 'A _____ difference' simply means there is statistical evidence that there is a difference; it does not mean the difference is necessarily large, important, or significant in the common meaning of the word.

The significance level of a test is a traditional frequentist statistical hypothesis testing concept.

a. Frequency distribution
b. Randomization
c. Standard deviation
d. Statistically significant

15. _____ is an advertisement in which a particular product specifically mentions a competitor by name for the express purpose of showing why the competitor is inferior to the product naming it.

This should not be confused with parody advertisements, where a fictional product is being advertised for the purpose of poking fun at the particular advertisement, nor should it be confused with the use of a coined brand name for the purpose of comparing the product without actually naming an actual competitor. ('Wikipedia tastes better and is less filling than the Encyclopedia Galactica.')

In the 1980s, during what has been referred to as the cola wars, soft-drink manufacturer Pepsi ran a series of advertisements where people, caught on hidden camera, in a blind taste test, chose Pepsi over rival Coca-Cola.

a. Cost per conversion
b. Comparative advertising
c. Heavy-up
d. GL-70

Chapter 24. Introducing Multivariate Statistical Analysis

1. _____ is a broad label that refers to any individuals or households that use goods and services generated within the economy. The concept of a _____ is used in different contexts, so that the usage and significance of the term may vary.

A _____ is a person who uses any product or service.

   a. 6-3-5 Brainwriting
   b. Power III
   c. Consumer
   d. 180SearchAssistant

2. _____ is defined by the American _____ Association as the activity, set of institutions, and processes for creating, communicating, delivering, and exchanging offerings that have value for customers, clients, partners, and society at large. The term developed from the original meaning which referred literally to going to market, as in shopping, or going to a market to sell goods or services.

_____ practice tends to be seen as a creative industry, which includes advertising, distribution and selling.

   a. Marketing
   b. Customer acquisition management
   c. Product naming
   d. Marketing myopia

3. Human beings are also considered to be _____ because they have the ability to change raw materials into valuable _____. The term Human _____ can also be defined as the skills, energies, talents, abilities and knowledge that are used for the production of goods or the rendering of services. While taking into account human beings as _____, the following things have to be kept in mind:

   - The size of the population
   - The capabilities of the individuals in that population

Many _____ cannot be consumed in their original form. They have to be processed in order to change them into more usable commodities.

   a. Power III
   b. 6-3-5 Brainwriting
   c. 180SearchAssistant
   d. Resources

4. The _____ is a publication of the United States Census Bureau, an agency of the United States Department of Commerce. Published annually since 1878, the statistics describe social and economic conditions in the United States.

In 1975 a two volume Historical Statistics of the United States, Colonial Times to 1970 Bicentennial Edition was published.

   a. Power III
   b. 180SearchAssistant
   c. 6-3-5 Brainwriting
   d. Statistical Abstract of the United States

5. The _____ is a professional association for marketers. As of 2008 it had approximately 40,000 members. There are collegiate chapters on 250 campuses.
   a. ACNielsen
   b. AMAX
   c. ADTECH
   d. American Marketing Association

Chapter 24. Introducing Multivariate Statistical Analysis

6. _____ is a branch of philosophy which seeks to address questions about morality, such as how a moral outcome can be achieved in a specific situation (applied _____), how moral values should be determined (normative _____), what moral values people actually abide by (descriptive _____), what the fundamental semantic, ontological, and epistemic nature of _____ or morality is (meta-_____), and how moral capacity or moral agency develops and what its nature is (moral psychology.)

Socrates was one of the first Greek philosophers to encourage both scholars and the common citizen to turn their attention from the outside world to the condition of man. In this view, Knowledge having a bearing on human life was placed highest, all other knowledge being secondary.

- a. ADTECH
- b. ACNielsen
- c. Ethics
- d. AMAX

7. In statistics, _____ is used for two things;

- to construct a simple formula that will predict what value will occur for a quantity of interest when other related variables take given values.
- to allow a test to be made of whether a given variable does have an effect on a quantity of interest in situations where there may be many related variables.

In both cases, several sets of outcomes are available for the quantity of interest together with the related variables.

_____ is a form of regression analysis in which the relationship between one or more independent variables and another variable, called the dependent variable, is modelled by a least squares function, called a _____ equation. This function is a linear combination of one or more model parameters, called regression coefficients. A _____ equation with one independent variable represents a straight line when the predicted value (i.e. the dependant variable from the regression equation) is plotted against the independent variable: this is called a simple _____.

- a. Heteroskedastic
- b. Sample size
- c. Descriptive statistics
- d. Linear regression

8. In statistics, _____ is a collective name for techniques for the modeling and analysis of numerical data consisting of values of a dependent variable and of one or more independent variables The dependent variable in the regression equation is modeled as a function of the independent variables, corresponding parameters, and an error term. The error term is treated as a random variable.

- a. Variance inflation factor
- b. Multicollinearity
- c. Stepwise regression
- d. Regression analysis

9. _____s are used in open sentences. For instance, in the formula x + 1 = 5, x is a _____ which represents an 'unknown' number. _____s are often represented by letters of the Roman alphabet, or those of other alphabets, such as Greek, and use other special symbols.

Chapter 24. Introducing Multivariate Statistical Analysis

a. Quantitative
c. Book of business
b. Personalization
d. Variable

10. In probability theory and statistics, _____ indicates the strength and direction of a linear relationship between two random variables. That is in contrast with the usage of the term in colloquial speech, denoting any relationship, not necessarily linear. In general statistical usage, _____ or co-relation refers to the departure of two random variables from independence.
    a. Frequency distribution
    c. Mean
    b. Probability
    d. Correlation

11. In statistics, the _____, R^2 is used in the context of statistical models whose main purpose is the prediction of future outcomes on the basis of other related information. It is the proportion of variability in a data set that is accounted for by the statistical model. It provides a measure of how well future outcomes are likely to be predicted by the model.
    a. Coefficient of determination
    c. Multicollinearity
    b. Variance inflation factor
    d. Regression analysis

12. The _____ of a test is a traditional frequentist statistical hypothesis testing concept. In simple cases, it is defined as the probability of making a decision to reject the null hypothesis when the null hypothesis is actually true (a decision known as a Type I error, or 'false positive determination'.) The decision is often made using the p-value: if the p-value is less than the _____, then the null hypothesis is rejected.
    a. Statistical hypothesis test
    c. Type I error
    b. Standard deviation
    d. Significance level

13. _____ is a statistical phenomenon in which two or more predictor variables in a multiple regression model are highly correlated. In this situation the coefficient estimates may change erratically in response to small changes in the model or the data. _____ does not reduce the predictive power or reliability of the model as a whole; it only affects calculations regarding individual predictors.
    a. Stepwise regression
    c. Variance inflation factor
    b. Multicollinearity
    d. Regression analysis

14. In statistics, analysis of variance (_____) is a collection of statistical models, and their associated procedures, in which the observed variance is partitioned into components due to different explanatory variables. In its simplest form _____ gives a statistical test of whether the means of several groups are all equal, and therefore generalizes Student's two-sample t-test to more than two groups.

There are three conceptual classes of such models:

1. Fixed-effects models assumes that the data came from normal populations which may differ only in their means. (Model 1)
2. Random effects models assume that the data describe a hierarchy of different populations whose differences are constrained by the hierarchy. (Model 2)
3. Mixed-effect models describe situations where both fixed and random effects are present. (Model 3)

Chapter 24. Introducing Multivariate Statistical Analysis

In practice, there are several types of _____ depending on the number of treatments and the way they are applied to the subjects in the experiment:

- One-way _____ is used to test for differences among two or more independent groups. Typically, however, the one-way _____ is used to test for differences among at least three groups, since the two-group case can be covered by a T-test (Gossett, 1908.)

a. ADTECH
c. ACNielsen
b. AMAX
d. ANOVA

15. In algebra, the _____ of a polynomial with real or complex coefficients is a certain expression in the coefficients of the polynomial which is equal to zero if and only if the polynomial has a multiple root (i.e. a root with multiplicity greater than one) in the complex numbers. For example, the _____ of the quadratic polynomial

$$ax^2 + bx + c \text{ is } b^2 - 4ac.$$

The _____ of the cubic polynomial

$$ax^3 + bx^2 + cx + d \text{ is } b^2c^2 - 4ac^3 - 4b^3d - 27a^2d^2 + 18abcd.$$

a. Consumption Map
c. Flighting
b. Lifestyle center
d. Discriminant

16. Linear _____ and the related Fisher's linear discriminant are methods used in statistics and machine learning to find the linear combination of features which best separate two or more classes of objects or events. The resulting combination may be used as a linear classifier, or, more commonly, for dimensionality reduction before later classification.

LDiscriminant analysis is closely related to ANOVA (analysis of variance) and regression analysis, which also attempt to express one dependent variable as a linear combination of other features or measurements.

a. Discriminant analysis
c. Linear discriminant analysis
b. Multiple discriminant analysis
d. Geodemographic segmentation

17. _____ is a measure of the strength of a brand, product, service relative to competitive offerings. There is often a geographic element to the competitive landscape. In defining _____, you must see to what extent a product, brand, or firm controls a product category in a given geographic area.

a. Market system
c. Discretionary spending
b. Productivity
d. Market dominance

18. _____ is a computer program used for statistical analysis.

Chapter 24. Introducing Multivariate Statistical Analysis

_____ (originally, Statistical Package for the Social Sciences) was released in its first version in 1968 after being founded by Norman Nie and C. Hadlai Hull. Nie was then a political science postgraduate at Stanford University,and now Research Professor in the Department of Political Science at Stanford and Professor Emeritus of Political Science at the University of Chicago.

a. Power III
b. 6-3-5 Brainwriting
c. 180SearchAssistant
d. SPSS

19. _____ is that part of statistical practice concerned with the selection of individual observations intended to yield some knowledge about a population of concern, especially for the purposes of statistical inference. Each observation measures one or more properties (weight, location, etc.) of an observable entity enumerated to distinguish objects or individuals.

a. Richard Buckminster 'Bucky' Fuller
b. Sampling
c. AStore
d. Sports Marketing Group

20. _____ is a telephone surveying technique in which the interviewer follows a script provided by a software application. The software is able to customize the flow of the questionnaire based on the answers provided, as well as information already known about the participant.

CATI may function in the following manner

- A computerized questionnaire is administered to respondents over the telephone.
- The interviewer sits in front of a computer screen
- Upon command, the computer dials the telephone number to be called.
- When contact is made, the interviewer reads the questions posed on the computer screen and records the respondent's answers directly into the computer.
- Interim and update reports can be compiled instantaneously, as the data are being collected.
- CATI software has built-in logic, which also enhances data accuracy.
- The program will personalize questions and control for logically incorrect answers, such as percentage answers that do not add up to 100 percent.
- The software has built-in branching logic, which will skip questions that are not applicable or will probe for more detail when warranted.

a. 6-3-5 Brainwriting
b. Power III
c. Computer-assisted telephone interviewing
d. 180SearchAssistant

21. _____ is a statistical method used to describe variability among observed variables in terms of fewer unobserved variables called factors. The observed variables are modeled as linear combinations of the factors, plus 'error' terms. The information gained about the interdependencies can be used later to reduce the set of variables in a dataset.

a. Power III
b. Factor analysis
c. Semantic differential
d. Likert scale

22. _____ refer to a collection of facts usually collected as the result of experience, observation or experiment or a set of premises. This may consist of numbers, words particularly as measurements or observations of a set of variables. _____ are often viewed as a lowest level of abstraction from which information and knowledge are derived.
   a. Data
   b. Mean
   c. Pearson product-moment correlation coefficient
   d. Sample size

23. '_____' is a class of statistical techniques that can be applied to data that exhibit 'natural' groupings. _____ sorts through the raw data and groups them into clusters. A cluster is a group of relatively homogeneous cases or observations.
   a. Structure mining
   b. 180SearchAssistant
   c. Cluster analysis
   d. Power III

24. _____ is a set of related statistical techniques often used in information visualization for exploring similarities or dissimilarities in data. MDS is a special case of ordination. An MDS algorithm starts with a matrix of item-item similarities, then assigns a location to each item in N-dimensional space, where N is specified a priori.
   a. Situational theory of publics
   b. Cocooning
   c. Convenience
   d. Multidimensional scaling

25. _____ is a mathematical science pertaining to the collection, analysis, interpretation or explanation, and presentation of data. It also provides tools for prediction and forecasting based on data. It is applicable to a wide variety of academic disciplines, from the natural and social sciences to the humanities, government and business.
   a. Type I error
   b. Median
   c. Statistics
   d. Null hypothesis

Chapter 25. Communicating Research Results: Research Report, Oral Presentation

1. _____ describes the situation when output from (or information about the result of) an event or phenomenon in the past will influence the same event/phenomenon in the present or future. When an event is part of a chain of cause-and-effect that forms a circuit or loop, then the event is said to 'feed back' into itself.

_____ is also a synonym for:

- _____ Signal; the information about the initial event that is the basis for subsequent modification of the event.
- _____ Loop; the causal path that leads from the initial generation of the _____ signal to the subsequent modification of the event.

_____ is a mechanism, process or signal that is looped back to control a system within itself. Such a loop is called a _____ loop.

a. 6-3-5 Brainwriting
b. Power III
c. 180SearchAssistant
d. Feedback

2. The U.S. _____ is an agency of the United States Department of Health and Human Services and is responsible for regulating and supervising the safety of foods, dietary supplements, drugs, vaccines, biological medical products, blood products, medical devices, radiation-emitting devices, veterinary products, and cosmetics. The FDA also enforces section 361 of the Public Health Service Act and the associated regulations, including sanitation requirements on interstate travel as well as specific rules for control of disease on products ranging from pet turtles to semen donations for assisted reproductive medicine techniques.

The FDA is an agency within the United States Department of Health and Human Services responsible for protecting and promoting the nation's public health.

a. 6-3-5 Brainwriting
b. 180SearchAssistant
c. Power III
d. Food and Drug Administration

3. _____ refer to a collection of facts usually collected as the result of experience, observation or experiment or a set of premises. This may consist of numbers, words particularly as measurements or observations of a set of variables. _____ are often viewed as a lowest level of abstraction from which information and knowledge are derived.
a. Data
b. Mean
c. Pearson product-moment correlation coefficient
d. Sample size

4. A _____ is the price one pays as remuneration for services, especially the honorarium paid to a doctor, lawyer, consultant, or other member of a learned profession. _____s usually allow for overhead, wages, costs, and markup.

Traditionally, professionals in Great Britain received a _____ in contradistinction to a payment, salary, or wage, and would often use guineas rather than pounds as units of account.

a. Transfer pricing
b. Price war
c. Price shading
d. Fee

Chapter 25. Communicating Research Results: Research Report, Oral Presentation

5. _____ is a measure of the strength of a brand, product, service relative to competitive offerings. There is often a geographic element to the competitive landscape. In defining _____, you must see to what extent a product, brand, or firm controls a product category in a given geographic area.

  a. Productivity
  b. Market dominance
  c. Market system
  d. Discretionary spending

6. The verb _____ or grant _____ means to give permission. The noun _____ refers to that permission as well as to the document memorializing that permission. _____ may be granted by a party to another party as an element of an agreement between those parties.

  a. Power III
  b. 6-3-5 Brainwriting
  c. License
  d. 180SearchAssistant

7. In statistics, analysis of variance (_____) is a collection of statistical models, and their associated procedures, in which the observed variance is partitioned into components due to different explanatory variables. In its simplest form _____ gives a statistical test of whether the means of several groups are all equal, and therefore generalizes Student's two-sample t-test to more than two groups.

There are three conceptual classes of such models:

  1. Fixed-effects models assumes that the data came from normal populations which may differ only in their means. (Model 1)
  2. Random effects models assume that the data describe a hierarchy of different populations whose differences are constrained by the hierarchy. (Model 2)
  3. Mixed-effect models describe situations where both fixed and random effects are present. (Model 3)

In practice, there are several types of _____ depending on the number of treatments and the way they are applied to the subjects in the experiment:

  - One-way _____ is used to test for differences among two or more independent groups. Typically, however, the one-way _____ is used to test for differences among at least three groups, since the two-group case can be covered by a T-test (Gossett, 1908.)

  a. ANOVA
  b. ADTECH
  c. ACNielsen
  d. AMAX

8. The _____ is a global navigation satellite system (GNSS) developed by the United States Department of Defense and managed by the United States Air Force 50th Space Wing. It is the only fully functional GNSS in the world, can be used freely, and is often used by civilians for navigation purposes. It uses a constellation of between 24 and 32 Medium Earth Orbit satellites that transmit precise microwave signals, which allow _____ receivers to determine their current location, the time, and their velocity.

  a. 180SearchAssistant
  b. 6-3-5 Brainwriting
  c. Power III
  d. Global positioning system

9. _____ is a mathematical science pertaining to the collection, analysis, interpretation or explanation, and presentation of data. It also provides tools for prediction and forecasting based on data. It is applicable to a wide variety of academic disciplines, from the natural and social sciences to the humanities, government and business.

Chapter 25. Communicating Research Results: Research Report, Oral Presentation

a. Null hypothesis
c. Median

b. Type I error
d. Statistics

10. _____ is a telephone surveying technique in which the interviewer follows a script provided by a software application. The software is able to customize the flow of the questionnaire based on the answers provided, as well as information already known about the participant.

CATI may function in the following manner

- A computerized questionnaire is administered to respondents over the telephone.
- The interviewer sits in front of a computer screen
- Upon command, the computer dials the telephone number to be called.
- When contact is made, the interviewer reads the questions posed on the computer screen and records the respondent's answers directly into the computer.
- Interim and update reports can be compiled instantaneously, as the data are being collected.
- CATI software has built-in logic, which also enhances data accuracy.
- The program will personalize questions and control for logically incorrect answers, such as percentage answers that do not add up to 100 percent.
- The software has built-in branching logic, which will skip questions that are not applicable or will probe for more detail when warranted.

a. 180SearchAssistant
c. Computer-assisted telephone interviewing

b. Power III
d. 6-3-5 Brainwriting

11. _____ is defined by the American _____ Association as the activity, set of institutions, and processes for creating, communicating, delivering, and exchanging offerings that have value for customers, clients, partners, and society at large. The term developed from the original meaning which referred literally to going to market, as in shopping, or going to a market to sell goods or services.

_____ practice tends to be seen as a creative industry, which includes advertising, distribution and selling.

a. Marketing myopia
c. Product naming

b. Customer acquisition management
d. Marketing

12. Consumer market research is a form of applied sociology that concentrates on understanding the behaviours, whims and preferences, of consumers in a market-based economy, and aims to understand the effects and comparative success of marketing campaigns. The field of consumer _____ as a statistical science was pioneered by Arthur Nielsen with the founding of the ACNielsen Company in 1923 .

Thus _____ is the systematic and objective identification, collection, analysis, and dissemination of information for the purpose of assisting management in decision making related to the identification and solution of problems and opportunities in marketing.

a. Focus group
c. Logit analysis
b. Marketing research process
d. Marketing research

13. The _____ is a publication of the United States Census Bureau, an agency of the United States Department of Commerce. Published annually since 1878, the statistics describe social and economic conditions in the United States.

In 1975 a two volume Historical Statistics of the United States, Colonial Times to 1970 Bicentennial Edition was published.

a. 180SearchAssistant
c. 6-3-5 Brainwriting
b. Power III
d. Statistical Abstract of the United States

14. A _____ is a psychometric scale commonly used in questionnaires, and is the most widely used scale in survey research. When responding to a Likert questionnaire item, respondents specify their level of agreement to a statement. The scale is named after its inventor, psychologist Rensis Likert.

a. Semantic differential
c. Power III
b. Likert scale
d. Factor analysis

15. In probability theory and statistics, _____ indicates the strength and direction of a linear relationship between two random variables. That is in contrast with the usage of the term in colloquial speech, denoting any relationship, not necessarily linear. In general statistical usage, _____ or co-relation refers to the departure of two random variables from independence.

a. Mean
c. Probability
b. Frequency distribution
d. Correlation

16. _____ is a contract between two parties, one being the employer and the other being the employee. An employee may be defined as: 'A person in the service of another under any contract of hire, express or implied, oral or written, where the employer has the power or right to control and direct the employee in the material details of how the work is to be performed.' Black's Law Dictionary page 471 (5th ed. 1979.)

a. ADTECH
c. ACNielsen
b. AMAX
d. Employment

17. A personal and cultural _____ is a relative ethic _____, an assumption upon which implementation can be extrapolated. A _____ system is a set of consistent _____s and measures that is soo not true. A principle _____ is a foundation upon which other _____s and measures of integrity are based.

a. Package-on-Package
c. Supreme Court of the United States
b. Value
d. Perceptual maps

18. _____ is the ability of an individual or group to seclude themselves or information about themselves and thereby reveal themselves selectively. The boundaries and content of what is considered private differ among cultures and individuals, but share basic common themes. _____ is sometimes related to anonymity, the wish to remain unnoticed or unidentified in the public realm.

a. Privacy
c. Power III
b. 6-3-5 Brainwriting
d. 180SearchAssistant

Chapter 25. Communicating Research Results: Research Report, Oral Presentation

19. In probability theory and statistics, the _____ is one of the most widely used theoretical probability distributions in inferential statistics, e.g., in statistical significance tests. It is useful because, under reasonable assumptions, easily calculated quantities can be proven to have distributions that approximate to the _____ if the null hypothesis is true.

The best-known situations in which the _____ are used are the common chi-square tests for goodness of fit of an observed distribution to a theoretical one, and of the independence of two criteria of classification of qualitative data.

a. Mystery shoppers
c. Chi-square distribution
b. Scientific controls
d. Second Life

20. _____ is one of the four elements of marketing mix. An organization or set of organizations (go-betweens) involved in the process of making a product or service available for use or consumption by a consumer or business user.

The other three parts of the marketing mix are product, pricing, and promotion.

a. Distribution
c. Japan Advertising Photographers' Association
b. Comparison-Shopping agent
d. Better Living Through Chemistry

21. The _____ of a test is a traditional frequentist statistical hypothesis testing concept. In simple cases, it is defined as the probability of making a decision to reject the null hypothesis when the null hypothesis is actually true (a decision known as a Type I error, or 'false positive determination'.) The decision is often made using the p-value: if the p-value is less than the _____, then the null hypothesis is rejected.

a. Significance level
c. Type I error
b. Standard deviation
d. Statistical hypothesis test

22. In statistics, the _____ is a common measure of the correlation (linear dependence) between two variables X and Y. It is very widely used in the sciences as a measure of the strength of linear dependence between two variables, giving a value somewhere between +1 and -1 inclusive. It was first introduced by Francis Galton in the 1880s, and named after Karl Pearson.

In accordance with the usual convention, when calculated for an entire population, the Pearson product-moment correlation is typically designated by the analogous Greek letter, which in this case is ρ.

a. Median
c. Standard deviation
b. Control chart
d. Pearson product-moment correlation coefficient

ANSWER KEY

Chapter 1
1. c	2. d	3. d	4. b	5. a	6. b	7. c	8. d	9. d	10. d
11. c	12. b	13. b	14. c	15. a	16. c	17. d	18. a	19. b	20. b
21. d	22. d	23. a	24. d	25. d	26. d	27. a			

Chapter 2
1. c	2. a	3. a	4. c	5. a	6. d	7. d	8. d	9. d	10. b
11. d	12. a	13. d	14. a	15. d	16. b	17. a	18. d	19. a	20. b
21. d	22. b	23. d	24. c	25. d	26. b	27. d	28. c		

Chapter 3
1. d	2. b	3. c	4. d	5. a	6. a	7. d	8. a	9. c	10. c
11. d	12. a	13. a	14. d	15. a	16. d	17. d	18. a	19. d	20. a
21. a	22. d	23. b	24. b						

Chapter 4
1. a	2. d	3. a	4. a	5. a	6. d	7. c	8. d	9. d	10. a
11. d	12. d	13. d	14. d	15. d	16. a	17. d	18. a	19. c	20. b
21. d	22. d	23. b	24. b	25. d	26. d	27. d	28. b	29. d	30. d
31. d	32. d	33. b	34. b	35. d	36. c	37. d	38. c	39. a	40. b
41. a									

Chapter 5
1. d	2. c	3. a	4. c	5. d	6. d	7. d	8. b	9. c	10. a
11. d	12. a	13. b	14. d	15. d	16. d				

Chapter 6
1. d	2. d	3. a	4. d	5. d	6. a	7. d	8. d	9. d	10. b
11. b	12. d	13. d	14. a	15. b	16. b	17. d	18. d	19. b	20. d
21. b	22. c	23. d							

Chapter 7
1. a	2. d	3. d	4. a	5. a	6. d	7. c	8. d	9. d	10. b
11. b	12. b	13. d	14. d	15. d	16. d	17. d	18. d	19. d	20. d
21. d	22. a								

Chapter 8
1. d	2. b	3. a	4. d	5. a	6. c	7. b	8. d	9. d	10. d
11. b	12. d	13. c	14. b	15. b	16. d				

Chapter 9
1. c	2. a	3. d	4. c	5. d	6. a	7. a	8. c	9. a	10. b
11. d	12. a	13. d	14. c						

ANSWER KEY

Chapter 10
1. c 2. c 3. d 4. b 5. d 6. d 7. d 8. a 9. c 10. d
11. b

Chapter 11
1. d 2. d 3. b 4. b 5. d 6. d 7. c 8. d 9. d 10. d
11. d 12. d 13. c 14. b 15. b 16. d 17. d 18. b 19. d 20. d
21. d 22. a 23. d 24. d 25. a 26. b

Chapter 12
1. d 2. b 3. c 4. a 5. d 6. b 7. c 8. d 9. d 10. b
11. c 12. b 13. c 14. a 15. b 16. b 17. d 18. d 19. d

Chapter 13
1. a 2. d 3. d 4. d 5. d 6. d 7. d 8. c 9. c 10. c
11. c 12. d 13. a 14. d 15. c 16. a 17. c 18. d 19. d 20. b
21. b

Chapter 14
1. c 2. d 3. b 4. b 5. c 6. a 7. d 8. d 9. b 10. d
11. a

Chapter 15
1. d 2. d 3. d 4. a 5. b 6. c 7. c 8. d 9. d 10. c
11. b 12. d 13. d 14. a 15. d 16. d 17. a 18. d 19. b 20. d
21. a 22. a 23. d 24. d 25. d

Chapter 16
1. d 2. a 3. c 4. d 5. b 6. b 7. b 8. d 9. a 10. d
11. d 12. a 13. b 14. d 15. d 16. b 17. b 18. d 19. d 20. c
21. c 22. a 23. d

Chapter 17
1. a 2. b 3. b 4. d 5. d 6. b 7. b 8. b 9. d 10. d
11. d 12. b 13. a 14. a 15. a 16. d 17. a 18. d 19. d 20. b
21. c 22. b 23. d 24. a 25. d 26. d 27. d 28. b 29. a 30. c
31. d

Chapter 18
1. a 2. d 3. c 4. d 5. a 6. d 7. a 8. d 9. d 10. d
11. d 12. d 13. a

ANSWER KEY

Chapter 19
1. a   2. d   3. d   4. d   5. d   6. d   7. d   8. c   9. d   10. a
11. d

Chapter 20
1. d   2. b   3. b   4. d   5. d   6. b   7. b   8. a   9. a   10. c
11. c   12. d   13. c

Chapter 21
1. d   2. d   3. d   4. b   5. c   6. d   7. c   8. c   9. d   10. d
11. a   12. d   13. d   14. a   15. a   16. d   17. d   18. d   19. d   20. d
21. a   22. a

Chapter 22
1. b   2. d   3. d   4. d   5. a   6. b   7. d   8. d   9. d   10. c
11. c   12. d

Chapter 23
1. d   2. b   3. a   4. b   5. d   6. b   7. c   8. a   9. b   10. d
11. b   12. d   13. b   14. d   15. b

Chapter 24
1. c   2. a   3. d   4. d   5. d   6. c   7. d   8. d   9. d   10. d
11. a   12. d   13. b   14. d   15. d   16. a   17. d   18. d   19. b   20. c
21. b   22. a   23. c   24. d   25. c

Chapter 25
1. d   2. d   3. a   4. d   5. b   6. c   7. a   8. d   9. d   10. c
11. d   12. d   13. d   14. b   15. d   16. d   17. b   18. a   19. c   20. a
21. a   22. d

www.ingramcontent.com/pod-product-compliance
Lightning Source LLC
Chambersburg PA
CBHW082043230426
43670CB00016B/2760